apr

WHEELS WEST

Overleaf: *In the 1850s Topeka, Kansas, was at the junction of the Santa Fe and Oregon trails, and it became an important railroad town when the Santa Fe Railway began building westward from this point in 1868. Shown here is Kansas Avenue in 1870.*

Right: *The plaza at Santa Fe was still the goal of wagon trains in 1861. Not even the Civil War could end the flow of trade over the Santa Fe Trail. The wagon trains kept rolling, bringing the Southwest closer to the ever-expanding Anglo-American frontier.*

WHEELS WEST
1590-1900

By RICHARD DUNLOP

Foreword by Ray Allen Billington

RAND MℂNALLY & COMPANY

CHICAGO · NEW YORK · SAN FRANCISCO

PHOTO CREDITS

American Museum of Natural History, p. 12; Amon Carter Museum of Western Art, pp. 115, 162; Association of American Railroads, p. 180 (top); Bancroft Library, p. 116; from *Beyond the Mississippi* by Albert D. Richardson (1867), p. 122; Black Hills, Badlands and Lakes Association, p. 106; Burlington Northern, p. 192; Church of Jesus Christ of Latter-day Saints, p. 66; Brad Cooper, p. 26; Robert Cromie, pp. 24, 25; Deadwood Chamber of Commerce, p. 104; Denver Public Library, Western History Department, pp. 23, 31, 41, 47, 57 (bottom), 62 (bottom), 63, 74, 75 (top), 83, 85, 87, 90, 91, 92, 93, 96–97, 98, 102, 114, 119, 124, 125, 127, 133, 141 (bottom), 142 (bottom), 144, 145, 148, 149, 163 (top), 166, 178 (bottom), 189 (bottom), 196, 197 (bottom); Howard R. Driggs, p. 82; Joan Dunlop, pp. 60, 135, 178 (top); from *The Golden State* by Guy McClellan (1874), p. 117; from *Harper's Weekly* (6-6-1857, 12-11-1858), pp. 77 (top), 131; from *History of the Express Business* by A. L. Stimson (1881), p. 130; Herman Jones, p. 132; Kansas State Historical Society, pp. 76, 167; from *Leslie's Illustrated* (9-1878), p. 174 (bottom); Library of Congress, pp. 15, 68, 84, 100, 141 (top), 156 (top), 193, 194 (top); Library, State Historical Society of Colorado, pp. 21, 28, 39, 42, 44, 45, 53, 54, 55, 64, 65, 73, 107, 111, 113, 120, 121, 123, 126, 128, 134, 147, 150, 151, 152–153, 154, 161 (top), 164, 168, 170, 171, 185 (top); G. T. Morrison, p. 20; Museum of New Mexico, Collections in the, p. 3; National Archives, pp. 16, 62 (top), 99; National Park Service, p. 57 (top); Nebraska State Historical Society, p. 77 (bottom); New Mexico State Tourist Bureau, p. 18; from *Our New West* by Samuel Bowles (1869), p. 80; Santa Fe Railway, pp. 1, 9, 30, 32, 35, 37, 38, 40, 105, 173 (top), 174 (top), 180 (bottom), 182 (bottom), 184, 185 (bottom), 186, 188, 190, 191 (top), 194 (bottom), 195; Smithsonian Institution, p. 187; Solomon D. Butcher Collection, Nebraska State Historical Society, p. 177 (top); South Dakota State Historical Society, pp. 94, 95, 108, 109, 163 (bottom), 176, 191 (bottom); Southern Pacific Railroad, p. 183; State of California, Division of Beaches and Parks, p. 142 (top); State Historical Society of North Dakota, pp. 173 (bottom), 175, 177 (bottom); State of Illinois, Department of Conservation, p. 86; Texas State Archives, p. 172; Title Insurance and Trust Company, Historical Collection, pp. 88, 197 (top); Union Pacific Railroad, pp. 75 (bottom), 182 (top); University of Oklahoma, Division of Manuscripts, p. 169; Utah State Historical Society, p. 67; Walters Art Gallery, p. 17; Wells Fargo Bank History Room, San Francisco, pp. 136, 146, 155, 161 (bottom); Wyoming Travel Commission, pp. 78, 81 (top).

Designed by MARIO PAGLIAI

Library of Congress Cataloging in Publication Data

Dunlop, Richard.
WHEELS WEST, 1590–1900.

Bibliography: p.
Includes index.
1. Coaching—The West—History. 2. Wagons—History.
3. The West—History. I. Title.
HE5629.D86   388.34′1′0978   77-6901
ISBN 0-528-81047-2

First Printing, 1977

CONTENTS

Foreword

TODAY, when we wing our way across the continent in a scant five hours as attractive hostesses ply us with food and drink, or when we speed across Wyoming at somewhat over the fifty-five-mile limit the law allows, we may forget that our pioneer ancestors braved untold hardships and suffered interminable months of torture to span those same distances. The modern automobile, even when restrained by legislative edict, can traverse in fifteen or twenty minutes the miles covered by a plodding wagon train in a whole day of weary travel. How those ancestors of ours, we may think, must have longed for speedier transportation as they inched along toward the dim western horizon while days stretched into weeks and weeks into months.

Such was far from the case. In the eyes of the pioneers, the vehicles that carried them westward were the crowning achievements in mankind's age-old battle to shrink distances—a battle that reached its zenith amidst the vast distances of the American West. The prairie schooners that provided transportation and shelter during their two months on the overland trail might seem jolting torture chambers to us today, but they assured their owners a safe and reasonably secure journey to the sunset edge of the continent where awaited prosperity and a chance to "grow up with the country." The ornate Concord coaches that spanned the 2,000 miles between Missouri and San Francisco in only twenty-four days are to us symbols of a leisurely age whose slow pace of life offers a peaceful contrast to the pressures of

the present, but to that generation they were the ultimate in luxury and death-defying speed. Man had begun the conquest of space, even if he still moved with tortoiselike speed by our standards.

This book tells the story of that age, and of the wheeled vehicles that allowed Americans to overcome the interminable distances of the Far West. It begins in the dawn-days of the continent, when an unsung Indian hero in Mexico, fashioning a toy dog for his youngster, devised ceramic disks that allowed the boy to pull the animal as he walked. It ends with Leland Stanford standing at Promontory, Utah, swinging a sledge (and missing) as he drove a golden spike into a laurel tie to complete the first transcontinental railroad. What monumental developments were encompassed between those two events!

Richard Dunlop describes them all, and brilliantly. He has written not just another history of western transportation (we have an abundance of those) but an account of the vehicles that allowed that transportation revolution to go on. They are all here: the cumbersome Mexican carretas whose unlubricated axles emitted such earsplitting squeaks that they could be heard a mile away; the sturdy wagons that helped Santa Fe traders achieve the nation's Manifest Destiny, including the canvas-covered prairie schooners that swept the tide of settlement westward to engulf the continent; the Red River carts that rolled out over the northern plains with their loads of foodstuffs and furs; the lumbering freighters that supplied scattered military posts and mining camps; the ornate stagecoaches that carried passengers and mail westward during the 1850s and 1860s to help cement the bonds of union between East and West. This is the heroic story that is superbly told and magnificently illustrated on the pages of this book.

But Richard Dunlop has done even more. All the familiar vehicles are paid proper attention—the Conestoga wagon, the Concord coach, the heavy-bodied freighter, the cattleman's chuck wagon—each is described in detail and each is awarded its proper place in history. But so, too, are less well known but sometimes even more important horse-drawn conveyances: the Murphy wagons that frustrated the attempt of New Mexican governors to collect excessive customs duties from Santa Fe traders; the Young wagons that brought an ingenious Negro justified fame; the dearborns and Jerseys that provided a degree of comfort for wagon-train bosses; the handcarts of the Mormons; the Dougherty spring wagons, called "ambulances" by the Army; the finely designed Studebakers with their axles of black hickory; the inelegant celerity wagons and mud wagons that carried overland travelers more miles than the Concord coaches.

There also are other vehicles that proved even Yankee ingenuity inadequate when faced by raw nature on the vast plains of the West: windwagons that sent their inventors' hopes soaring until they themselves soared into the air before a sudden gust of wind, or crashed their drivers into hidden gullies; a gigantic steam contraption with wheels twelve feet across that never overcame its mechanical problems; and others just as weird. Not until another equally improbable invention—the steam locomotive—came west was the age of horsepower doomed.

This book, however, is more than a descriptive catalogue of western transportation. Richard Dunlop has combed hundreds of government reports, overland diaries, journals, and reminiscences—some of them unpublished—to view western travel as the travelers themselves saw it. Here is a fresh perspective on transportation, and a fresh insight into the pleasures and discomforts that passengers experienced on the trail. But beyond all this, he has also unearthed a whole libraryful of delicious anecdotes to enliven his narrative and assure readers pleasure as well as profit. This is a memorable book, rich in history and lore, but above all a treasure trove for the mind and a feast for the eye. Read, and look, and enjoy.

Ray Allen Billington
THE HUNTINGTON LIBRARY

Right: *Trinidad, Colorado, was first a trading post on the Mountain Branch of the Santa Fe Trail. By 1878, when this picture was taken, it was a trading center with board sidewalks and a well-known hotel, the Baca House, which still stands on the town's main street.*

WHEELS WEST

Introduction

ARCHAEOLOGISTS DIGGING into the Olmec past at Las Remojadas, Mexico, near Veracruz, came upon a pottery dog, unmistakably a Chihuahua. Judging from the axles upon which the figure stood, it was meant to roll on wheels. This was a simple discovery, but to Americanists all over the world it was almost unbelievable. They had grown up professionally in the certainty that the wheel had never rolled in North America before the Spaniards came. Not long afterwards ceramic wheels were found at another Olmec site nearby. They fitted exactly onto the axles on the toy dog.

The toy Chihuahua, now in the American Museum of Natural History in New York City, continues to provoke contention among archaeologists. Some, the diffusionists, claim that the concept of the wheel must have been brought from Europe or Asia by pre-Columbian transoceanic travelers. Others are just as confident that the toy dog is proof that the wheel was invented separately in the New World.

The most important thing is not whether the wheel is indigenous to New World cultures, but rather why it apparently was never put to work as a mode of transportation. Dr. Michael E. Moseley, associate curator of Middle and South American Archaeology and Ethnology at Chicago's Field Museum and one of the most brilliant of young Americanists, points out that ceramic wheels have also been found in the Peruvian cultures, but the people of those advanced South American civilizations were content to transport their burdens on the backs of llamas, on their own backs, or, in the case of the prodigious blocks of stone from which they fashioned their remarkable structures, on sledges. If this had not been the case, the humble Spanish carreta, the Red River cart of the northern fur traders, the Conestoga and Murphy wagons of the freighters, and the prairie schooners of the emigrants never would have been such a significant factor in the opening of the trans-Mississippi American West to white exploration and settlement. They gave white settlers an extraordinary advantage.

In 1817 Johann Christian Ginzrot published a now rare book, the German title of which can be translated as "The Carriages and Vehicles of the Greeks and Romans and Other Peoples of the Antique World," in which he claimed that Adam invented the carriage. Archaeologists digging in the Middle East have long since proven Ginzrot wrong. Mesopotamian ceramics found at the Tell Halaf site in northern Syria, dating to 4000 B.C., depict wheeled carts. The Sumerians of 3500 B.C. transported their agricultural products and religious objects in wheeled vehicles. A four-wheel covered wagon unearthed at Tepe Gawra, near Mosul, Iraq, dates from the third millennium B.C.; it resembles the prairie schooners of the American West.

Significantly, E. A. Speiser, who discovered the covered wagon, believed that it was a foreign type from beyond the Caspian Sea. This fits in with theories that man first domesticated the ox, the wild ass, and the horse as draft animals in the vast heartland

A pottery toy animal dating from the Late Classic period—from 800 to 1200 A.D.—was dug from an Olmec site at Las Remojadas, near Veracruz, Mexico. The toy bears some resemblance to a deer but is actually a dog, representing the ancestor of the Chihuahua. The toy figure was crafted centuries before the Spanish brought the wheel to the New World, yet it was mounted on axles. At another Olmec site nearby, archaeologists soon discovered ceramic wheels that fitted exactly onto the axles. The toy animal, now in the American Museum of Natural History in New York City, continues to stir up controversy. Was it intended for a religious purpose or for a child to play with? Did its ancient Indian makers copy the wheel from trans-Atlantic sources, or did they invent it independently? Other wheeled toys have been found in both Mexico and Peru, but the Indians did not use the wheel for transportation.

of Central Asia. The nomads of Central Asia, perhaps as early as the fifth millennium B.C., very probably invented the wheel. This is supposition, however, for the earliest proven use of the wheel was in Mesopotamia.

How did the wheel originate? Some authorities claim that it first was a cult symbol representing the sun. The spokes of wheels shown in early Mesopotamian artifacts can be likened to the sun's rays. In the New World the circle of the wheel stood for the sun in the religions of the Indians of Mexico and the Indians of the Great Plains. Recently, when I spent some time among the Hunkpapa Sioux, I heard David Fast Horse, a wise old religious leader, explain how the magic circle of the teepee and of the sky and the horizon enclosed the circle of humanity gathered around a council fire. The concept of the wheel was as much a symbol of pre-Columbian Indian religious beliefs as it was of Mesopotamian beliefs of thousands of years ago.

"The significant thing is that the Indian society did not have the motivation to use the wheel for transportation," says Dr. Moseley. "A source of power is needed to make wheels and axle worthwhile, and this was lacking."

The nomads of Central Asia and the nomads of North America both placed heavy loads on boughs lopped from trees to pull them across the plains. The Asian nomads made a slide car from two poles tied together so that such draft animals as dogs, reindeer, horses, and oxen could pull it. In 1540 Francisco Vázquez de Coronado saw the American Indians on the southern high plains using a similar slide car. The early French explorers, who also saw the slide car in use, called it a "travois." On the travois Plains Indians transported supplies, teepees, children, the sick, and the old. It was commonly a webbing supported on two long poles with shafts for a woman or dog, and later for the horse when that animal became a part of their way of life.

The sledge of Central Asia was given four wheels to cut down on friction and became a crude wagon. The slide car would only have needed two wheels at the ends of the poles to become a sort of cart or chariot. The nomads of the Central Asia plains adopted the wheel, but the nomads of the North American plains did not. According to Dr. Moseley the reason for this is that in Asia there were easily tamed draft animals, while in North America there were only the dog, which lacked the necessary strength, and the fractious buffalo. Nor would the Indian women, who often had to do heavy labor, have taken kindly to pulling carts.

Once the Spanish introduced the horse to the Indians, they adapted it quickly into their way of life. The Shoshoni and Bannock of southern Idaho were using the horse by 1700, and by 1800 they were among the most remarkable mounted nomads the world has known. The Plains Indians also took to the horse, which proved just as much at home on the North American steppes as it had been on its ancestral steppes in Asia.

The Indians did not adapt the wheel to their culture, but on the plains they made the horse an integral part of their way of life. Indians such as this Sioux chief depicted by Frederic Remington were some of the finest horsemen the world has known. It was the Spanish who introduced horses, as well as wheeled transportation, to the Indians. The three-toed horse was native to the Americas, but it was long since extinct when the Indians fashioned their first travois. Thus pre-Columbian Indians did not have horses to ride or to pull their vehicles. Yet on a ranch in the Black Mesa of Oklahoma there is a recently discovered Iberian Punic inscription done before 200 B.C., which has been identified by Dr. Barry Fell of Harvard University, and twenty feet from the inscription is a carved horse that bears a Punic brand mark and the name "Swift Runner" in Punic script. "Swift Runner" may have raced over the North American plains carrying a trans-Atlantic stranger—no one knows from where—more than 1,700 years before the Spanish brought horses to the New World.

The horse changed the Indians' life-style, but they did not think of harnessing it to wheeled vehicles. Locked in their traditional way of life, they found the white man's wagons incomprehensible. A friendly Indian walked along beside the Donner Party and called out "Gee, haw, whoa" in puzzled imitation of the oxen's drivers. A wagon abandoned in the face of a Kansas blizzard by a trading party on the Santa Fe Trail had vanished when the men came back in the spring. The Pawnee had taken the wagon. Indian squaws made harnesses for themselves from strips of buffalo hide and pulled the wagon around from camp to camp to give small children a ride. As far as the Indians were concerned, it was just an object to amuse children.

When 1,200 Cheyenne, Arapaho, and Sioux captured eight huge freight wagons near Fort Rankin, Colorado, in 1865, they threw most of the contents out on the prairie because they could not carry so many items away on travois. They loaded hundreds of bushels of corn, sacks of flour and sugar, cases of canned goods, bales of clothing, bolts of cloth, and cases of shoes onto travois, but these represented only a fraction of the valuable goods they had captured. They finally chained the oxen to the wagons and attempted to drive them as part of a herd of cattle across the prairie. This failed to work, however, and they soon gave up their effort to put the white man's wheel into use.

Even late in the nineteenth century, on their frontier with the whites, the Indians found the wheel a strange thing. In the Battle of Apache Pass in Arizona, the Apache first encountered howitzers mounted on wheels. They were defeated. Afterwards Chief Cochise said, "You would never have beaten us if you had not shot wagons at us."

The defeated chief's remark and the failure of the victorious Indians in Colorado to master the freight wagons are only two of hundreds of examples of the Indians' significant inability to understand or utilize the wheel.

Wheeled vehicles, direct descendants of the primitive carts and wagons of Central Asia, opened up the American West to the greatest influx of settlement the world has known. *Wheels West* is the story of wheeled vehicles drawn ever westward behind plodding oxen, cantankerous mules, and spirited horses. The keel could carry the frontier up the Mississippi and the Missouri rivers, but from there on west the frontier rolled on the wheel. It was a progress that the Indians could only watch with fascination and, doubtless, anguish.

Right: *As the Anglo-American frontier rolled forward on the wheel, the Indians could only look on with a combination of fascination and, doubtless, anguish. Pioneer painter Alfred Jacob Miller shows Pawnee Indians watching a westering caravan of the 1830s from a rugged vantage point.*

Below: *The great days of a nomadic people following the buffalo herds across the plains drew to an end as the U.S. Army settled the Indians on reservations. To help them make the transition to their new life, the Army issued supplies to the once proud people who had become government wards. The Indians shown in this photograph are waiting for food staples to be distributed at Camp Supply in the Indian Territory. Indians still had not accepted the wagon, and they loaded the white man's handouts onto travois to haul them away to their villages. Finally the Army began to give the Indians wagons, which were specially made for them by such firms as Studebaker.*

Gypsum sands billow in vast dunes at the White Sands National Monument in southern New Mexico. In 1936 a desert sandstorm shifted the dunes and excavated a Spanish carreta that had been buried by another storm centuries before. It brought to light rough timbers and broken wheels that had rolled down the trails when the Spanish Empire was expanding into what is now the American Southwest.

ACROSS THE RIO GRANDE

THE WIND can do the painstaking work of the archaeologist. It can unveil a mystery of the past.

That afternoon on the New Mexico desert the breeze freshened into a blow that flattened the sage before it and sent the tumbleweed whirling. At the White Sands National Monument it lifted particles of gypsum sand and threw them scattershot. By dusk the blow had become a gale, and the white sand swirled down the long dunes, seeming to stand erect in human form, then stooping and bending as if peering into the shadows. At times like this the wind and the sand create what Mexicans call the *Palo Blanco*, the ghost of a beautiful woman. According to Tom Charles, who became the first superintendent when the White Sands were made a national monument in 1933, she "comes dressed in the flowing white robes of her wedding gown and looks and searches for her lover lost and buried in the Great White Sands."

The wind became a raging sandstorm. Even the tiny white mice that live in the sands kept to their burrows. Ranchers kept to their dwellings. During that night and the next day whole dunes shifted their positions.

When the sun could at last be seen again, Watson Ritch, who had lived near the northwest corner of the sands for fifty-six years, came out of his ranch house to discover a strange world. Landmarks had vanished. Then a remarkable thing caught his eye—a dark object out on the sands where no object had ever been seen before. He walked over to investigate it. He stared in disbelief. With incredible precision the wind had dug into the sand and thrown it aside to reveal a primitive vehicle. The wheels were hand-hewn. There was the axle. There were the tongue of the cart and part of the body. It was a Spanish carreta that had been overwhelmed by another sandstorm, centuries ago, as it trundled along the treacherous trail.

Where had the cart come from? Where was it going? Nobody could be sure. Some experts told Ritch that it had been passing along the west side of the sands on its way from Spanish El Paso to the flats west of Tularosa to seek a load of salt. Others said it had been following a fateful shortcut on the route to Santa Fe and had lost its way in the storm.

An ox yoke was also laid bare by the wind, but there was no sign of the oxen that had pulled the carreta. If the driver was the lost lover of the *Palo Blanco*, she must go on searching for him, because there was no sign of him either. Apparently driver and oxen had escaped the storm or lay buried elsewhere beneath the strange shifting sands.

The carreta was excavated by the wind in 1936. Ritch, the son of former Gov. William G. Ritch of New Mexico Territory, kept the cart until 1959, when his wife lent it to the National Park Service so that it could be put on display at White Sands National Monument headquarters. In 1975 William G. Ritch, Watson Ritch's son, donated the relic of the past unearthed by the wind to the monument, where it still may be seen.

Above: *The carreta excavated by the wind at the White Sands National Monument was found by Watson Ritch, son of William G. Ritch, former governor of New Mexico Territory. Watson's son donated the relic to the National Park Service museum at the monument. Its timbers and wheels, fashioned out of solid sections of wood, remind visitors of the Spanish past.*

Right: *During the nineteenth century Indians of the southwestern pueblos were trained by the Spanish to accept the carreta as a means of transport.*

In December of 1959 I came to the White Sands National Monument and saw the cart in the lee of the headquarters, awaiting exhibition. I ran my hands over its rough timbers and looked at its wheels, which had been shaped out of solid sections of wood. The Spanish past of the American Southwest became more tangible to me because of this vehicle.

A carreta was never anything much to look at. The American explorer Stephen H. Long, searching the southernmost portions of the Louisiana Purchase in 1820, came across trails left by carts such as this. In 1845 Lt. James W. Abert of the U.S. Army, on an exploration of the headwaters of the Arkansas River, reported that the rough Spanish road along the Canadian River was strewn with broken axletrees from Mexican carts. In his "Report on the Upper Arkansas" he wrote about finding a cart abandoned intact. He described what he found:

"Two eccentric wheels, not exactly circular, formed by sawing off the ends of large logs, and rimming them with pieces of timber to increase their diameter. They were perforated in the neighborhood of the centre, to receive an axletree of cottonwood. A suitable pole, and a little square box of wicker wood completed the laughable machine."

To the young lieutenant, blessed with no small measure of Anglo-American superiority, the carreta was indeed laughable, but these humble vehicles had borne the commerce of the vast Spanish empire in the New World. The clumsy carretas were without question the first wheeled vehicles to roll into what is now the United States.

On July 27, 1590, some fifty years after Francisco Vázquez de Coronado had returned from his empty search for the Seven Cities of Cibola, Gaspar Castaño de Sosa, lieutenant governor of Nuevo León, set out with 170 men, women, and children from Nuevo Almadén on a colonizing expedition beyond the Rio Grande. Their goods were piled high in carretas drawn by oxen. On September 9, according to the manuscript of his "Memoria" in the Real Academia de la Historia in Madrid, Castaño de Sosa's carretas—the first wheeled vehicles to enter

what became the United States—reached the Rio Grande. There is a difference of opinion as to exactly where the traders crossed the river. Vito Alessio Robles, a prominent Mexican historian, believes that the crossing was made at Los Chizos Ford, now in Big Bend National Park.

Some historians disagree with Alessio Robles. They believe instead that Castaño de Sosa and his expedition crossed the Rio Grande in the vicinity of Villa Acuna, downriver from Del Rio. Castaño de Sosa's manuscript is inexact, not because he was a bad navigator, but because he was traveling in unmapped territory. Wheels rolled into the southwestern wilderness before any maps of the area were drawn.

One fact emerges clearly from reading the Castaño de Sosa manuscript. The big cart in which he placed great store broke down in a ravine on September 1, before he reached the Rio Grande, and the vehicles that crossed into Texas and rolled past the Devils River and on to the Salado River were carretas similar to the one dug by the wind from the White Sands dunes. One cart contained a coffer for the royal fifth of the profits in gold and silver that Castaño de Sosa, with the inimitable optimism of the Spanish *conquistadores,* was confident he would bring back with him. As a Spanish official, he was prepared to present his king with the fifth share due to him by law. The cart bearing the royal coffer broke down at the Salado River, but Castaño de Sosa managed to repair it so that it could bump and thump over the bare plains of West Texas. Despite this momentary victory, Castaño de Sosa's expedition ended in failure. How many of his carretas were abandoned on the high plains and how many returned safely to Mexico is not known.

If Alessio Robles is correct, Los Chizos Ford is one of the most historic spots in the United States. A few years ago, while on a float trip in a rubber raft down the Rio Grande, I paused at the ford with a party of park rangers and visitors. There is still no bridge at this crossing, although grinning Mexican boys perch people on burros for a small fee and lead them through the shallow rippling waters to the far bank. Obscure as this historic border crossing may be, it has been a legitimate port of entry into the United States since 1895, when William Ferguson, a U.S. Treasury agent, arrived there and established a post.

Ferguson wrote home: "Nowhere else have I found such a wildly weird country. A man grows watchful, awestruck by nature in her lofty moods. Emotions are stirred by the grandeur of the scenery and the ever-changing play of light and shadow."

The Chisos Mountains on either side of the Rio Grande's Big Bend were called by the Spanish, *hechizos,* meaning "enchanted." Let the shadows lengthen and the last light shine on the bald rock outcroppings so that they become spectral sentinels, and the country is still enchanted today. Standing at the crossing, one can easily imagine Castaño de Sosa and his men driving their oxen into the water. The oxen pulled wheeled vehicles over the sand and rocks of the river bottom to their first landfall on what was to be American soil.

The carreta that Castaño de Sosa brought to Texas and that later was used by other Spaniards in New Mexico, Arizona, and California as well was not invented in the New World. "Carreta" is a Spanish derivative of the Latin *carreta,* a diminutive of *carrus* for "cart," and the carreta may have been used in Spain as long ago as Roman times.

My wife Joan and I, while on a research trip to Spain, left Madrid and flew to the far northwestern region of Galicia, to the north of Portugal. We had learned that the carreta is still in common use there. The morning after our arrival in the ancient pilgrimage town of Santiago de Compostela, where the body of Saint James is said to be preserved beneath the altar of the cathedral, we set out on a bus into the countryside. We had scarcely quit the town when we came upon the first carreta. Pulled by plodding oxen, it was rolling along the shoulder of the macadam highway. It was loaded with vegetables being taken to the market, and sitting on the produce were five or six young Galician children, their rosy cheeks, freckles, and russet or sandy hair proof of their Celtic blood. The Galician people share a common ancestry with the Gaelic people of Ireland and Scotland and speak a similar language. They have lived in the misty mountains of northwest Spain, which are clad in heather like those of Scotland, since as far back as 1800 B.C. Even the gold ornaments unearthed in ancient Galician graves resemble in design the early Irish gold jewelry on display at Trinity College in Dublin.

The children shrilled a greeting and waved at our bus. Everywhere we drove in Galicia over the next several days, we saw functioning carretas identical to the vehicle yielded up by the White Sands in New Mexico.

One night at our hotel, the Hotel de los Reyes Católicos—which, by the way, was founded by Ferdinand and Isabella—we talked to historian Maria Luz Lago Artime. Despite her Spanish-sounding name, she is pure auburn-haired Celtic. She kicked off her shoes to show us how to dance the muineira. Arms aloft, she skipped nimbly through the paces of what Scots would call a Highland fling. She talked of the Galician people, who still speak their old tongue in their homes and keep alive their kinship with the Gaelic peoples of the British Isles, and she talked of the carreta.

"We brought the carreta to the New World," she proudly said.

The roads of Galicia lead down to salt water, for it is bounded on the north by the Bay of Biscay and on the west by the Atlantic. It is no wonder that these westernmost people of Spain, who live close to the sea and are possessed of the Celt's roving spirit, made up a high percentage of the Spanish emigrants to the New World. Who can deny that the first carreta manufactured in the New World may have been fashioned by Galician instead of perhaps Castilian hands? Given the high percentage of emigrants from Galicia, this may well have been the case. Certainly the carreta still rolls along the roads of Galicia, as it does along the back roads of Mexico.

In the New World and the Old the Spanish carreta could be heard coming while still miles away, since its wooden wheels turned on wooden axles. William Watts Hart Davis, a U.S. attorney in New Mexico Territory in the 1850s, wrote, "The wheels are never greased, and as they are driven along they make an unearthly sound—being a respectable tenor for a double-bass horse fiddle."

To Davis and to most other people the carts were painfully noisy, but to the cart driver the screeching of the wheels was music to his ears. The friction of axletree and linchpins made a satisfying scream that kept evil spirits away in the night. In the mountains of Spain and the mountains of the American Southwest it warned wagon trains coming from opposite directions on the narrow roads to pull over at a place wide enough for the two trains to pass. In Galicia carters even watered the axletree to make the cart sing in a louder voice. The translation of an old Galician cart song runs:

> If you want your cart to sing,
> Wet the axle in the river.
> When it is sodden,
> It will sound like a pipe.

"Pipe" to a Galician means a bagpipe, and critics of Gaelic bagpipe music may indeed find something of a comparison.

Many Galician towns, grown tired of squeaking wheels, required that a carter put grease on his axle to cut down the noise. The carter obeyed the law while in town, but once he was out of town he scraped off the grease and poured water over the axle or smeared it with resin, so that once again the turning wheels could make the earsplitting sounds that were so satisfying to his ears.

In the American Southwest there was usually a shortage of lubricant, and the carter could always claim that there was nothing he could do about the racket he made. Actually this was not the case, for any carter knew that if he fed the tender leaves of the prickly pear into the wheel housing, they would lubricate the turning wheels very nicely.

Not until eight years after the Castaño de Sosa expedition, according to known records, did the Spanish carreta make a second intrusion into the virtually trackless land across the Rio Grande. Then, on January 26, 1598, Don Juan de Oñate gathered together eighty-three carretas and a large party of men, women, and children and set out to establish a settlement, which he was to call Santa Fe. Those women and children who were too weak to walk rode

To the old plaza at Santa Fe wagonloads of wood were brought from the mountains for sale during the nineteenth century. The winter chill of northern New Mexico kept the wood wagons rolling through the snows to replenish the fires that were warming the hearths of the city.

atop the goods in the carts. The men rigged covers over them as protection against the wind and the sun. Oñate's silks and jewels reposed in a silver bathtub in one of the carts, for he had no intention of starting life in New Mexico on a shoestring.

When the carts crossed streams, the men drove their horses into the current. The carretas bobbed like corks in the flood. Each driver stood on the wagon tongue and cracked his whip over the backs of his horses, which finally dragged the cart out on the other bank. Oñate was able to get his carretas across the streams by using this method, but he ran into trouble with the flock of sheep that accompanied the expedition. When his party reached the Conchos River, which was swollen by winter rains, the sheep absolutely refused to enter the surging water. Gaspar Perez de Villagia, a youth in the party, later wrote down an account of how Oñate solved the problem:

"He ordered that two dozen of the largest cart wheels be brought. These he securely anchored to rafts, two across, the entire width of the river. He then ordered that the tall trees which grew along the river banks be cut and trimmed and taking the longest and strongest branches, we laid these length-wise and crosswise, over the cart wheels, covering them with branches, bark, and earth."

The pontoon bridge supported on cart wheels worked very well, and the sheep crossed over the torrent in safety.

The Spanish carreta used in the American Southwest usually rolled on two wheels, but sometimes it rode on four. It was made without nails or iron, and the frame was often fastened together with rawhide. A surviving carreta now in the Roscoe E. Hazard collection of vehicles at Seeley Stables in the Old Town State Historic Park at San Diego, California, was originally fastened together with wooden pegs, although bolts were added during a renovation before the cart was acquired by the Hazard collection.

As a rule cottonwood made up the box of the cart, but the axle was fashioned of pecan or live oak. A carreta might be as much as fifteen feet long and six feet wide, and if the load was balanced nicely on its single axle, it could carry up to 5,000 pounds of cargo in its bed. William Heath Davis, an early

Anglo-American resident of Spanish and Mexican California, described the carts which the rancheros used to haul hides and tallow down to the trading ships that anchored at San Diego and Monterey:

"The body of the vehicle was set on the axles, having no springs, but with four wheels (the smaller wagons with two) sawed out of a tree four feet in diameter, and about a foot thick, a solid block or section, with a hole in the middle for the axle. Sticks were set up perpendicularly along the sides and covered with hides stretched across them, thus inclosing the body of the wagon."

A carreta's wheels might be cut out of any durable wood. The carts used by Castaño de Sosa had wheels fashioned from thick cross sections of cottonwood logs. Later carreta makers preferred oak for their wheels. By artful joining of sections solid wheels were built, which might be seven feet in diameter. Two long boards running through the sides held together as many as five separate pieces, as in the case of two carreta wheels, about 200 years old, now in the Hazard collection.

Mexican freighters attempting the dangerous trails of the Southwest favored such huge wheels,

Left: *South of San Antonio, Texas, the Spanish established five missions, each a day's journey by creaking oxcart from the other. Visitors to Mission San José find a sturdy carreta standing on the grounds as a memento of wheeled transportation in the days when padres were attempting to make Christians out of Indian neophytes.*

Below: *The wheels of the carreta at Mission San José are similar in construction to those of earlier carts but they are rimmed with iron, a proof that they are of more recent vintage.*

A carreta bearing a statue of Saint Michael to New Mexico in 1683 became stuck in the mud as it rolled down the Rio Grande Valley. The people took this as a sign that the saint wanted to stay, and they founded the Socorro Mission. The statue may still be seen adorning the altar of the church. At Christmas time luminarias outline the mission, one of three in the valley below El Paso.

for they could jounce in and out of the deep ruts and potholes with relative impunity. This suited the Apache, implacable foes of the traders. They sometimes captured a carter and tied him upside down to his seven-foot wagon wheel. This left his head a convenient one foot off the ground. The Apache built small fires beneath the hapless trader and boiled his brain until it burst out of his skull.

The hazards of the trail were many. Las Cruces, New Mexico, is named for the crosses set up to mark the graves of oxcart drivers murdered by the Indians. Socorro, Texas, was founded in a less sanguinary way. According to legend a carreta carrying a statue of Saint Michael stuck in the mud left by a Rio Grande flood, and settlers took this as a sign that the saint wanted to remain where he was. They built the mission in which the now 300-year-old statue is enshrined.

The people of the Southwest used carretas for many purposes. The Spaniards and Mexicans hauled cannons in them to frontier presidios. In 1795, when the Spanish established the Castillo Guijarros on the east side of Point Loma near the entrance to San Diego Bay on the California coast, the existing settlement at Santa Barbara sent enough axletrees and wheels for ten carts as its contribution to the strength of the fort. Thirty-five years later, in 1830, Lt. Col. José Francisco Ruiz led a detachment of Mexican cavalry from San Antonio de Bexar to the point where El Camino Real crossed the Brazos River of Texas; on this occasion a heavy carreta carried along not only a cannon, but also ammunition and a blacksmith's forge. The carreta went in the vanguard of Spanish and Mexican civilization.

On feast days villagers placed a skeleton known as the "angel of death" in a carreta. The skeleton held a bow and arrow or a musket in his bony fingers. Josiah Gregg, an indefatigable chronicler of the frontier Southwest, observed on his trips to Santa Fe and beyond that the clumsy carretas were also "the pleasure-carriages of the rancheros whose families are conveyed in them to the towns, whether to market or the fiestas, or on other joyful occasions."

According to William Heath Davis, the rancheros of California converted the carreta into a vehicle for pleasure: "Families sometimes took long journeys in these wagons fitted up with more style, the sides being lined with calico or sheeting, or even light silk, with mattresses on the floor of the wagon. With cooking and eating arrangements they went along comfortable, camping by a spring, and sleeping in the wagon, traveling days at a time."

Such a comfortable and relatively luxurious carreta is a far cry from the crude vehicle discovered by Lieutenant Abert on the banks of the Canadian River. In California a ranchero's daughters and their Indian maidservants regularly packed picnic lunches, piled the week's washing of clothes and sheets into an ox-drawn carreta, and rode down through the fields to the spring or stream where they could scrub the clothes and then take a joyful dip in the cooling waters.

For the most part carretas were put to more workaday use. When Joseph Magoffin built his still-standing house at Magoffinsville on the Rio Grande, which was to metamorphose into modern-day El Paso, men hauled the timber on creaking carts down from the forested mountains. Mexican traders, their carretas piled high with goods, came over the Santa Fe Trail to Missouri, even as Anglo-American traders carried goods along the trail to Santa Fe. After the Anglo-American frontier engulfed the Spanish Southwest, the carreta was still used to carry supplies and freight to mining camps and other isolated settlements. George Wilkins Kendall, a sheepherder of Post Oak Springs, Texas, during the American Civil War, loaded 18,000 pounds of wool into Mexican carretas and hauled it eastward to New Orleans.

The most significant function of the carreta in the settlement of the Southwest was its use in the supply trains that came from Mexico to frontier missions ranging from Texas to California. Every three years after 1617, when the service was started, caravans of carts driven by Indians and escorted by soldiers undertook the arduous journey to the frontier. It was a long trek; a caravan going from Central Mexico to Tucson, Arizona, for example, might take six months. One year when the winter was particularly severe, the carts crossed the Rio Grande on ice.

It was to trade with the Comanche and other Plains Indians that the carretas made their deepest penetration towards the westering frontier of the Anglo-Americans. The carts of the Comancheros—men who traded with the southwestern Indians—and also the ciboleros—buffalo hunters—blazed the trails and rough roads that Anglo-American explorers found when they reached the high plains

of the Southwest in the early nineteenth century. Zebulon Montgomery Pike, during his exploration of 1806, came upon Spanish roads as far east as Kansas. Not only did the Comancheros trade with the Comanche, but they also bartered far to the north with such tribes as the Kiowa, Sioux, Cheyenne, Arapaho, Crow, Ute, and Shoshoni.

The carretas of the Spanish Comancheros did not begin to roll out onto the high plains of North America until after 1786, when peace was made between the Spanish and the Comanche. The Comancheros were redoubtable people. Their carts carried such things as sacks of freshly baked bread, for a single sack of which the Comanche would gladly give a pony. What other things the carretas carried can be learned from studying the oddments that the Comancheros traded to the Comanche to ransom Anglo-American captives, whom they could sell back later to the Americans. In March, 1850, traders from Mora bought a twelve-year-old boy for four knives, one plug of tobacco, two fanegas of corn, six yards of red Indian cloth, and four blankets. Another twelve-year-old boy cost one mare, one rifle, one shirt, one pair of drawers, thirty packages of powder, some bullets, and one buffalo robe. A young woman purchased by the Comancheros cost two striped blankets, ten yards of blue cotton drilling, ten yards of calico, ten yards of cotton sheeting, two kerchiefs, four plugs of tobacco, one bag of corn, and one knife.

The ciboleros also often carried trade goods with them on their outward-bound trips onto the plains, but they hauled buffalo meat back with them. When they had killed their buffalo, they cut razor-thin slices of meat and dried them either in the hot southwestern sun or over fires made from pieces of dry dung, known as buffalo chips. They packed the jerked meat into the carretas by stamping it down with their bare feet, and strapped the hides on top.

Since there might be as many as fifty carretas in a hunting party, it is not surprising that the Plains Indians finally began to attack the ciboleros in order to keep them from decimating the dwindling buffalo herds. This became particularly true after the Civil War, when the ciboleros traded in their traditional carts for larger American wagons, which by then were becoming plentiful in the Southwest. The Comancheros also began to use the larger American wagons; backed by unscrupulous Americans, they turned to trading guns and whiskey to the Indians, thereby providing the now angered warriors with weapons for attacking the ciboleros.

The last major expansion of North America's Spanish-speaking population moved northwards into Colorado in carretas. In 1851 six Mexican families loaded their household goods in carretas and founded a new settlement at San Luis, the first town in the territory. Mexicans founded other towns in Colorado too, and carretas, many of which now had spoked wheels, were used over the early roads that tied them together.

A later expansion of Spanish-language people also moved northward in carretas. Six Mexican families loaded all their goods into carretas in 1851 to journey into Colorado and establish San Luis, the first town in the territory. Other Mexican towns were founded in Colorado, and the carreta became a popular vehicle on the roads that connected them.

As on the Anglo-American frontier, a man could always get a lively discussion going in the Southwest as to the best draft animals to haul the ubiquitous carreta. Without a doubt oxen came first and were always generally favored, but Oñate employed horses to pull his carts, and still others used mules. In California, where oxen were preferred, William Heath Davis wrote that "the wagons were drawn by oxen, with a nearly straight yoke fitting the top of the neck just back of the horns, and fastened with a piece of soft hide, and attached thereto and to the wagon."

In New Mexico as many as five or six span of oxen for each carreta were lashed to their wooden yokes by rawhide straps. As for the mules that pulled Mexican carretas, these were observed by Gregg to have uncommonly hard hoofs because of the arid climate. They could travel for weeks and months without shoes and did not seem to have the obstinate dispositions of the mules that were bred in the United States.

The carreta was always the sturdy vehicle upon which transportation in the Spanish Southwest depended, but there also were a few horse-drawn coaches owned by the very rich. A few public stages were operated by Mexicans after the coming of the Anglo-Americans. Employing the Mexican hitch used south of the border, these stagecoaches were drawn by six mules. Two were placed at the pole, and four were in the lead. The Mexican hitch was often used on the Mountain Branch of the Santa Fe Trail and on other New Mexico runs—to the great disgust of American drivers, who referred to the mules or horses hitched in such a fashion as "them damned three cornered teams."

Today more modern vehicles have largely replaced the stagecoaches and carretas of the American Southwest, but if a person travels to the small villages of New Mexico, he may find a few carretas still in use, their wheels still setting up a fearful scream as they go about the humble tasks that have been assigned to them since the first of their kind rolled across the Rio Grande in 1590.

WAGONS TO SANTA FE

THE INDIANS of the Great Plains overheard the bullwhackers driving their teams over the Santa Fe Trail. As a result they added two new words to their vocabulary—*whoa-haws* for "cattle," and *goddam* for "wagon." The white men always seemed to drive at the top of their voices, but let the "goddams" get stuck in the quicksand of a river crossing and they shouted at the "whoa-haws" with a fervor that aroused great wonder in the tribesmen listening from cover nearby.

Many people mistakenly believe that all the "goddams" driven to Santa Fe were Conestogas. In actuality only a small percentage of the wagons used on the Santa Fe Trail were Pennsylvania wagons, made either in the Pennsylvania Dutch counties of eastern Pennsylvania or, later on, in Pittsburgh. Most of them were Murphy or Espenscheidt wagons built in Saint Louis or Young wagons made in Independence, Missouri, and many were farm wagons of indeterminable parentage, manufactured in this small town or that in the American Midwest.

It is at least clear that when William Becknell started for Santa Fe from Franklin, Missouri, on May 22, 1822, with nearly thirty men and three farm wagons loaded with $5,000 worth of trading goods, he was taking the first wagons over the trail. Becknell, a onetime trapper and Indian trader who knew the plains well, employed double spans of mules to pull his wagons, and he double-teamed them to get his wagons through the sands of the Arkansas River.

Becknell pioneered the Cimarron Cutoff between the Arkansas River and San Miguel, a shorter and more level route than that through Raton Pass in the mountains. Crossing the *jornada* of the Cimarron, the thirsty men tipped their mules' ears to suck the blood and drank water from a buffalo's belly in order to survive. They also killed their dogs for meat. The trip proved to be worth the hardship; when Becknell reached Santa Fe, he was able to sell his goods for $15,000. When word of his profit reached Missouri, others began to load their wagons to go to Santa Fe, regardless of the difficulties that the trail might hold for them. They learned to live by the maxim that in the Cimarron, "even the jackrabbits carried three days' rations and a canteen of water."

Over the next few years carts and dearborn wagons and various road wagons were used on the trail, but it was the stout Conestoga—one of the most superb vehicles ever built on the North American continent—that captured the imagination. The ancestors of the Conestoga were the two-wheeled cart of the German Rhineland and the English road wagon. German emigrants, who came to be called the Pennsylvania Dutch, built the first Conestoga wagon on the shores of Conestoga Creek in Lancaster County in the early eighteenth century. It was a crude vehicle. The wheels were disks sawed from buttonwood or gum trees. As ironsmiths and wheelwrights improved, so did the wagons, and by the 1750s they were known throughout the thirteen

Old Santa Fe at the sunset end of the Santa Fe Trail lured the traders across the plains and through the mountains. William Becknell started from Franklin, Missouri, on May 22, 1822, with three farm wagons loaded with $5,000 worth of trading goods. These were the first wagons to take the Santa Fe Trail.

colonies for their quality and strength. Each year saw the wagons grow larger too; in time they reached a length of twenty-six feet and a height of eleven feet.

Seymour Dunbar's *A History of Travel in America* provides an apt description of the wagon that for generations was in the vanguard of commerce and settlement on the American frontier:

A Conestoga wagon was a huge affair, very heavily built, with a bed higher at each end than in the middle, and topped by a dull-white cloth cover which had a similar curve of still more pronounced degree. The wagon bed was constructed in concave shape in order that its contents might not spill out when it was going up or down hill. Still another distinguishing characteristic of the conveyance was its color. The underbody was always painted blue,

and the upper woodwork was invariably bright red. This chromatic scheme was as inevitable for every Conestoga wagon as though it had been prescribed by law with a penalty for refusal so to decorate.

As the years passed, Conestoga wagons were being made not only in Lancaster County, but also in the other Pennsylvania Dutch counties of Bucks, Berks, Chester, and York. One year Lancaster County alone had five wheelwrights, thirteen blacksmiths, twenty joiners, and seven turners working on the wagons. Each wagon was almost entirely hand-tooled. The frame of the boat-shaped bed was fashioned out of white oak. The boards were made of oak or poplar, and they were at least half an inch thick. A chain and staple secured the endgates, which could be dropped for loading and unloading. The wagon bed was well braced with iron, and the boards attached to the frame were fastened by rivets that were handmade.

The Conestoga has been called a "posey basket on wheels" because of its graceful white top of homespun or canvas. From six to thirteen hoops, depending on the size of the wagon, were stapled to the sideboards. The canopy, which might stretch to twenty-four feet, was roped to the sideboards and stretched tight over the end bows.

The wagonmakers knew that axles and hubs were critical. Wheelwrights shaped the hubs of split-resistant black or sour gum to the most exacting specifications. Axles and bolsters were fashioned out of oak or hickory wood, which is noted for its toughness. Wheel spokes and felloes were just as sturdily built, because no part of the running gear could be weaker than the other parts. There was no nut to keep the wheel from falling off. Instead a linchpin was dropped through an iron ring at the edge of the hub. This worked very well when the pin was new, but a worn linchpin would often drop out when the wagon jarred on a rock. Then the axle dragged on the ground, which could be vexing.

Real know-how was involved in the design of the wheels and axles. The axle must be shaped and the wheels dished just right to help take up the shock of jouncing over rutted roads under a heavy load. To make the spokes incline outward from the hub at the correct angle for maximum resilience and strength, mortises in both the hub and the inside of the felloes had to be cut with an exactness that was the test of any wheelwright's art.

The width of the rim varied from two to ten inches, depending on the kind of country in which the wagon was to be used. The muddier the road, the wider the rim required. Over the rim was fitted an iron tire, usually made of two sections a half inch thick. It was perfectly tailored to the size of the wheel and then welded together at both joints.

Fitting the iron tire over the rim was the blacksmith's task. He built a fire around the tire. When he determined that the iron was hot enough, he lifted the tire off with a pair of tongs, slid it over the wooden wheel, and knocked it into place with a mallet. The smith then poured cold water over the hot iron so that it shrank to fit the wheel. Let the iron be too hot, and it would char and weaken the wheel. Let it not be hot enough, and the fit would be loose. If the iron cooled too quickly, its grip would split the rim.

The front wheels, when finally fitted to the axle, were about three and a half feet high, and the rear

A linchpin firmly held the wheel onto a covered wagon's axle, at least until the linchpin became worn.

wheels were from four to five feet in height. The big wheels helped keep the load out of the water when the wagon forded a stream, and they easily rolled over rocks.

The blacksmith made other important contributions to a Conestoga wagon. He made brake shafts, linchpins, staples, latches, and hooks. He made stay chains of hand-forged links to hold the tailgate in place. He built the often ornate toolbox that would ride on the left side of the wagon just behind the lazy board, which was just behind the left front wheel. He might also hammer out a strip of steel that was inlaid lengthwise into the axle to make it wear longer. He made a decorated socket for the axe, which was standard equipment for any wagon. The feedbox, which was attached to the side of the wagon, gave him an opportunity to create something of fancy ironwork that was both useful and beautiful to look at.

The jack was deemed a critical piece of equipment. The blacksmith who made the iron tires for the wagon usually made the jack as well. The date of the wagon's manufacture and the manufacturer's initials were often cut into the pillar of the jack. This was a point of honor. Woe to the wagoner who borrowed another's jack and did not return it as soon as he was finished with it. A jack was needed when the wagoner had to replace a wheel that had popped off on the road when a linchpin dropped out, and also when he had to remove the wheels to grease the axles and bearing parts with pine-tar lubricant from the tar bucket that hung from a hook over the rear axle, next to the feedbox and water bucket. The tar, in addition to its use as a lubricant, could also be daubed on the wounds of both man and beast to keep away blowflies.

The driver of a Conestoga wagon might walk beside his team of three span of horses, ride the left

During the heyday of the Santa Fe Trail, the point of departure for trading expeditions was Independence, Missouri. Life in the frontier town revolved around its courthouse, which was crowned with a weather vane. The streets of Independence were made dusty by all manner of vehicles, but it was the great caravans of freight wagons that struck fire to the imaginations of townspeople and wagon masters alike.

wheelhorse, or sit on the lazy board, which could be pulled out from beneath the wagon bed in back of the left front wheel. The Conestoga driver made it the American preference to drive from the left side of a vehicle and to keep to the right side of the road, a custom that is observed by auto drivers to this day.

If he were seated on the lazy board, the driver might operate the cumbersome brake himself. Otherwise a teenaged boy, known to the Pennsylvania Dutch as *der shparr boo,* pulled the brake lever. When the driver or his boy heaved with all his might on the brake, the brake blocks pressed against the wheels.

John Strohm, writing in the U.S. Agricultural Report for 1863, described the impression made by a Conestoga wagon pulled by a team of splendid Conestoga horses:

These wagons and teams attracted attention and commanded admiration wherever they appeared. . . . The harness was constructed of the best materials, with an eye to show as well as utility. In the harness and trimmings of these teams [the owners] frequently indulged in expenses that approached extravagance. . . .

It was, indeed, an animating sight to see five or six highly fed horses, half covered with heavy bear skins, or decorated with gaudily fringed housings, surmounted with a set of finely toned bells, their bridles adorned with loops of red trimming, and moving over the ground with a brisk elastic step, snorting disdainfully at surrounding objects, as if half conscious of their superior appearance, and participating in the pride that swelled the bosom of their master and driver.

The "finely toned" bells that hung from the horses made a merry jinglejangle as the wagon rolled down the road. If a wagon got stuck in a mudhole, which happened all too frequently on prairie stretches of the Santa Fe Trail, and in river sands, it was often necessary for a team from another wagon to help pull the stuck wagon out. Then it was customary for the driver of the mired wagon to surrender his bells to the team that rescued him.

"I'll be there with bells on," a feisty driver would tell another if he wanted to let him know that he would reach a certain place on time in full jingling glory. Today Americans invited to a party use the same expression to let everybody understand that they will arrive rigged out in their best and ready for fun.

Conestoga drivers were a rough-and-ready lot, and they were renowned for their fondness for hard liquor. Frontiersmen told the story of the driver who sent his brake boy into a trading post to buy bread and whiskey. The boy returned with two loaves of bread and two bottles of whiskey. The driver cuffed him for bringing back "too much bread and too little whiskey."

A freighter to Santa Fe found it convenient indeed to buy a dozen bottles of whiskey for $4 apiece on the Missouri frontier. On the way he could drink the contents and trade each of the empty bottles in New Mexico for produce worth $6. For that matter, a wagon that cost $150 in Missouri would bring upwards of $500 in Santa Fe.

Anybody who has ever been asked to mind his p's and q's can claim kinship with these hard-drinking men, as well as with wagon drivers in Old England. They stopped for a mug of ale at the very few taverns along the road. Their wagons may have been heavy, but their pockets were light, so the tavern keeper put down on the cuff each pint or quart of ale consumed.

When a driver threatened to drink beyond his credit, the barkeep would warn, "Mind your pints and quarts. Mind your p's and q's." And English-speaking people have been minding their p's and q's ever since.

The Conestoga drivers smoked pencil-sized cigars bought at the price of four for a penny. The cigars were as strong as they were cheap. At first they were called "Conestogas" after the wagons, and then simply "stogies." A cigar that is both cheap and strong is still called a stogie.

Whether he was a mule skinner or a bull-whacker, a driver could be heard far down the trail by the crack of his whip. The whip gave him the power to flick hair and blood from the flank of any beast that didn't oblige him, but a good driver never laid a whip to his animals. Just the crack was enough to encourage them to make every effort. An ox respected a bullwhacker's whip. Made from a tough ash or pecan sapling, it was nearly ten feet long and had a lash just a trifle shorter but two inches in diameter, ending in a buckskin thong. The whip could also be used to kill any rattlesnakes that ventured within range.

The driver commanded his team with a firm hand on the jerk line. One long pull signaled the animals to turn left; a few short jerks, to turn right. He borrowed his vocal commands from the English countrymen who had settled in America. *Haw* meant "turn left"; *gee* meant "turn right"; and *whoa,* of course, meant "stop."

Some drivers were noted for the precise control they exerted over their teams with vocal commands. A wagoner who was particularly proud of this skill

might wager with others that he could lie on his back in a field and, with verbal orders alone, direct his team to pull the wagon over his body without harm. This often proved to be a foolhardy boast to make.

It was up to the wheelers to set the pace for the rest of the team and to provide braking power on a downhill grade when needed. If the grade was very steep, the driver might link a chain through the wheels and around the coupling poles to provide a brake.

Susan Shelby Magoffin, traveling over the Santa Fe Trail with her husband Samuel in 1846, commented in her diary about the formidableness of the wagons used on the trail, after spending a day on its Mountain Branch: "It takes a dozen men to steady a wagon with all its wheels locked—and for one who is some distance off to hear the crash it makes over the stones, is truly alarming. Till I rode ahead and understood the business, I supposed that every wagon had fallen over a precipice."

At first the wagons used on the Santa Fe Trail were farm wagons, Conestoga wagons, or Missouri-made copies of the Conestoga, but later much larger Murphy wagons took their place. This was due to the rapacity of New Mexico's Mexican governor,

Manuel Armijo. In 1839 Armijo imposed a tax of $500 on each American wagon entering Santa Fe. The traders complained, but Armijo would not listen. Joseph Murphy, a Saint Louis wagonmaker, saw his opportunity.

"We'll give the furrin' bandit a run for his money," he reportedly said, and he set about building enormous wagons that would carry prodigious loads. They would enable the traders to spread the wagon tax over a much larger quantity of goods.

Buffalo Bill Cody left a description of Murphy wagons, which he drove several decades later on the western frontier:

"The wagons were known as the 'J. Murphy wagon,' made at St. Louis especially for the plains business. They were very large and were strongly built, being capable of carrying seven thousand pounds of freight each. The wagon-boxes were very commodious—being as large as the rooms of an ordinary house—and were covered with two heavy canvas sheets to protect the merchandise from the rain."

Writing sixty years after the first huge wagon was built, Murphy's son Anselm remarked that "the height of the bed was such that a man standing inside would barely disclose the top of his head."

Left: *Josiah Gregg rode over the Santa Fe Trail. This illustration, taken from his epochal* Commerce of the Prairies, *shows the entrance of the traders into Santa Fe. Gregg describes the scene:* "Crowds of women and boys flocked around to see the new-comers; while crowds of léperos hung about, as usual, to see what they could pilfer. The wagoners were by no means free from excitement on this occasion. Informed of the ordeal they had to pass, they had spent the previous morning in rubbing up; and now they were prepared, with clean faces, sleek-combed hair, and their choicest Sunday suit to meet the fair eyes of glistening black that were sure to stare at them as they passed. There was yet another preparation to be made in order to show off to advantage. Each wagoner must tie a brand new cracker to the lash of his whip; for on driving through the streets and the plaza publica every one strives to outvie his comrades in the dexterity with which he flourishes this favorite badge of his authority."

Below: *The pioneer in homespun or deerskin trudging behind the white-topped wagons and the outrider with his rifle slung across his saddle ready for action captured the imagination of the eastern public, and artists soon were creating romantic portrayals of what life was like with a wagon train on the road to Santa Fe.*

Clarence H. Schultz, National Park Service historian at the Museum of Westward Expansion in Saint Louis, adds that "the rear wheel was seven feet in diameter with a felloe eight inches wide without a tire, as iron of such dimensions was unobtainable in 1839–1840. The sides of the wagon box were approximately five and one-half feet high. The tongue was of standard length but when hitched to four yoke of oxen, the effective length of the string would be fifty feet."

The wagon box had a Conestoga curved bottom.

Joseph Murphy, whose factory made at least 200,000 wagons for the western trails, was an Irish immigrant. In 1819 he became an apprentice to Daniel Caster, a Saint Louis wagonmaker. He worked for Caster for six years.

Young Murphy built his first wagon for the Santa Fe trade in 1827. It was a small vehicle, and he sold it to Jacob Jarrett for twenty-seven dollars. This money so pleased Murphy that he set about building another wagon, and then another and yet another.

Murphy hired German-born workmen, who brought the same care to the wagons they made in Saint Louis that the Pennsylvania Dutch brought to the Conestoga wagons. Murphy himself selected the seasoned timber for his wagons. He used only young saplings for the spokes. He made the axles of wood, since iron cracked under the torment of the Santa Fe Trail.

Murphy not only chose seasoned wood, but he also used a hot iron to drill bolt holes a little smaller in size than the bolts. His use of the hot iron instead of an auger prevented the wood from cracking around the bolts.

When a Murphy wagon was finished, it was loaded onto a riverboat at the Saint Louis levee, together with the goods it was to transport to Santa Fe. The boat brought the cargo to Blue Mills Landing at Independence, where a cement plant now stands. There the wagons rolled ashore to begin their life on the road to Santa Fe.

Other sturdy wagons that were prized on the Santa Fe Trail were made right in Independence. The best-known of the Independence wagonmakers was the Weston blacksmith shop, which stood on what is now the corner of Kansas and Liberty streets. It was a low brick building with outlying sheds, in which both white and black workers not only made new vehicles, but also reconditioned old ones. In an inferno of metal ringing on metal and flaring fires, the blacksmiths forged wagon tires, kingbolts, and linchpins. Among the fine wagonmakers at the Weston blacksmith shop was Hiram Young, a free Negro. Later on Young went into business for himself. The Young wagons were counted among the best on the Santa Fe Trail.

Still another frontier wagonmaker of note was situated in Arrow Rock, Missouri, a village which is now preserved as a state historic site. Traveling along the Santa Fe Trail with my family, I stopped at Templeton's blacksmith shop in the village. The smith pointed a plowshare on his anvil. He showed how he weighted horseshoes to keep a horse from knocking its heels together, and how to use a dunce cap to band a wagon wheel. He explained that his smithy was once one of the wagon shops that built wagons for the trail to Santa Fe. On a hot summer day Templeton's blacksmith shop blazes with heat, but I value it as a reminder of the days when wagons set out across the plains on trading adventures.

As the years passed, light wagons such as the dearborn and the Jersey were introduced. The Jersey wagon was a straight-sided wagon with four supports for the canvas roof. There were roll-up side curtains and an open seat outside with a footboard for the driver. The dearborn and the Jersey rode at the head of a column of wagons. Sometimes the wagon master would bring along an ambulance, a light prairie wagon, to carry provisions and provide transport for anybody who became ill. Two or three paying passengers might ride in the ambulance.

It was a colorful life. The caravans of wagons gathered at Council Grove, Kansas. When the morning of the departure came, the wagons were divided into two to four divisions for the march, with a lieutenant heading each division.

"Stretch out! Stretch out!" cried the captain of the train.

The drivers snapped their "Missouri pistols," long saplings with a lash ending in a buckskin thong. The wagons took their places in the line. The caravan began to roll, stirring up a cloud of dust. Outriders dashed ahead on horseback to dig out stream banks, so that the wagons could cross more easily. The long column of wagons pressed on towards the sunset end of the trail. Sometimes there were only a few dozen wagons in a company, but often there were many more. Josiah Gregg's company of 1831 had nearly 100 wagons, merchandise worth $200,000, and two cannons mounted upon carriages. The number of wagons crossing the prairies to Santa Fe grew every year. In 1846, 363 wagons carried $1 million in trade. In 1858, 1,-

Every year the number of wagons crossing the prairies to Santa Fe grew. In 1858, 1,827 wagons took the trail. In 1862, 3,000 wagons rolled west to Santa Fe, and in 1866 there were over 6,000 wagons. The trail divided so that some wagons went to the right over the Mountain Branch and crossed Raton Pass, while others took the Cimarron Cutoff, a route so dry and thirsty that it was said, "Even the jackrabbits carried three days' rations and a canteen of water."

827 wagons took the trail to Santa Fe. In 1862, 3,000 wagons carried goods worth $40 million. In 1866 there were at least 6,000 wagons.

The wagons made their way through fire and flood. If a prairie fire swept over the plains, there would be no trouble if the wind was blowing the fire away from the wagons, since it would burn slowly back against the wind, even through tall grass, and the wagons could easily escape. If the wind drove the fire towards a wagon, however, it would often consume both the wagon and the team.

Flood was a danger too. Wagon drivers raised the boxes with chocks to lift their cargoes above water level when they splashed through a ford. One driver halted his Pennsylvania wagon on the banks of a flooded stream. Chunks of ice were floating down the river. He chinked the box with snow and doused it with water, which froze and made it watertight. Thus the wagon became a boat and crossed the stream safely.

Quicksand was treacherous. The Cimarron Crossing of the Arkansas, which had given Becknell such difficulty, continued to menace wagons. The water was shallow, but the current was strong and wide, and the bottom was full of sinkholes. If a wagon stopped, it sank to the hubs in moments. The draft animals panicked. Sometimes a train took a whole day to cross the river, and after most trains had crossed, trade fabrics could be seen spread out on the sand hills to dry.

There was mud. Let a wagon stuck in the mud be overtaken by a sharp freeze, and it was often held there until the next thaw. There was the hot, dry air and the burning sun shining relentlessly. During a long hot spell, wood would shrink and crack, and felloes would pull apart. Iron tires would drop off rims. A spare axle might be needed at any time. Most of the spare axles were cut from hickories and oaks growing at Council Grove, rough-hewn for use in an emergency.

Above: *Susan Shelby Magoffin, wife of a successful Santa Fe trader, rode over the trail in 1846. She wrote of Council Grove in her diary: "It is a thick cluster of trees some miles in length through which runs a small creek called Council Grove Creek. There is a quantity of fine timber consisting of oaks, hickory, walnut etc. Each company coming out generally stop here a day or so to repair their wagons, rest the stock, get timbers for the remainder of the journey...."* Council Grove began as a jumping-off point for the wilderness to the west and grew into a prosperous town with stores and hotels of brick.

Right: *This rare picture of Kit Carson at the age of sixteen shows the famous scout one year after he was apprenticed to saddlemaker David Workman in Franklin, Missouri. Kit soon ran away with a freight caravan bound for Santa Fe. Workman advertised in an 1826 issue of the* Missouri Intelligencer: *"I will pay 1¢ for the return of the apprentice, Kit Carson, who ran away from my harness shop in Franklin, Mo. He is 16, small for his age, and has light hair."*

"It is a thick cluster of trees some miles in length," Susan Magoffin wrote of Council Grove, "through which runs a small creek called Council Grove Creek. There is a quantity of fine timber consisting of oaks, hickory, walnut etc. Each company coming out generally stop here a day or so to repair their wagons, rest the stock, get timbers for the remainder of the journey; these are lashed under the wagons."

There were also the Indians, who had formed a marked antipathy for "whoa-haws" and "goddams." At first the caravans traveled single file, strung out for as much as a mile. When wagon masters discovered just how vulnerable such a caravan was to Indian attack, they took to traveling in four sections once they passed Council Grove, each abreast of the other so that they could quickly form a hollow square for defense. They always formed such a square, or corral, at night. In a camp corral, the wagon tongues were usually pointed out of the circle. In a fighting corral, the wagon tongues were pointed inside the circle.

A train of twenty-five wagons en route over the Santa Fe Trail from Fort Leavenworth, Kansas, to Fort Union, New Mexico, was corralled when a Sioux raiding party appeared. Carpenter, the herder, was captured. The Sioux tied him to a pole and used him for bow and arrow practice, hoping to tempt his friends out of the corral of wagons so that they could be attacked. In 1847 Plains Indians killed forty-seven travelers over the Santa Fe Trail, destroyed 330 wagons, and stole 6,500 draft animals. At the height of their depredations the Cimarron Cutoff was all but closed.

A wagon was more than a vehicle of transportation. It was a source of valuable objects that could

save lives, as the story of Andrew Broadus illustrates. When Broadus, a driver with a train joined by a runaway sixteen-year-old boy named Kit Carson, saw a wolf close by, he yanked his gun from the tail of his wagon. The trigger caught and the gun went off, firing a ball into his forearm. The arm was shattered. In his book *Kit Carson* Stanley Vestal reports what happened next.

"It'll have to come off," said the wagon master, who knew that the arm would putrefy in the heat.

At first Broadus refused, but when blood poisoning streaked up his arm and death drew near, he begged somebody to cut off the limb. Apparently nobody could steel himself for the task.

"I kin do it," offered young Kit.

"Y're too young, Kit. Let somebody else do it," said a hunter.

A teamster got out a rusty handsaw and filed teeth on its back for cutting the bone. The men built a hot fire, then took a kingbolt from one of the wagons and heated it. After he severed the arm, the hunter cauterized the raw stump with the white-hot bolt. Then he rubbed cool axle grease over the wound and bandaged it. Broadus recovered.

Not many horses were used to pull freight wagons over the Santa Fe Trail. Not only were horses more expensive, but feed for them had to be carried on the train. Insects pestered a horse more, and impure water was more likely to give it distemper.

Mules and oxen were favored. Mule skinners and bullwhackers were always at loggerheads as to which draft animal was the best. In 1829 Maj. Bennett Riley, commanding the first American military escort over the trail, used oxen to pull his wagons. These were the first oxen on the trail. During the same year Charles Bent used oxen on a wagon train to Santa Fe. Soon bullwhackers were claiming that oxen were more manageable and were not so easily frightened by the calamities of the trail. They didn't require as much grazing ground and were cheaper to buy. In case of extreme need, they could be slaughtered and eaten with more satisfaction than could a mule.

A bull outfit was not exactly swift on the trail. James Pritchard measured the progress of his train with a watch and surveyor's chain and discovered that the cruising speed of an ox-drawn wagon on firm surfaces was about three miles per hour. Let the road get rough, and the pace slackened. On the average, a bull outfit would cover about twenty miles in ten hours, which included an hour break at noon.

Dependable and uncomplaining, an ox was a faithful friend to a bullwhacker. A man always mourned the loss of an ox, but who ever mourned for a mule?

A mule skinner had to admit the cantankerous nature of his favorites, but he could point out that an ox's feet were tender and difficult to shoe. No ox shoes could stand the long trail to Santa Fe, and it was often necessary to tie sacks made from cowhide or buffalo skin over the oxen's feet to help protect them. As for shoeing an ox, it was an ordeal for man and beast. A shallow trench was dug, and the animal was turned upside down in it. Only then could the blacksmith get at the hoofs, since an ox cannot stand on three legs.

"Have you ever seen oxen stampeding to a water hole?" a mule skinner would ask. "Mules have more sense."

A bullwhacker need only yoke a young ox between two leaders and two wheelers, and it would soon get the hang of its job and fall to with a will. Breaking a mule to harness, on the other hand, was

Above: *Oxen and mules were the preferred draft animals on the Santa Fe Trail. All kinds of wagons, carriages, and carts could be encountered on the long trail that stretched "from civilization to sundown," as the pioneers poetically put it.*

Right: *David Wood's Magnolia Route, which originated at his home station in Montrose, linked together Colorado freight destinations. Wood favored mules to pull his wagons. A "hee-haw minstrel," as wagoners called a mule, was tough and durable and could drink alkali water with relative impunity. Mules were easier to shoe than oxen, and their hoofs were so tough that they could go unshod if need be, although their feet might then be worn so smooth that they would slip on steep hills.*

invariably a confrontation of the most violent sort. Lewis H. Garrard, who went west at the age of seventeen in July, 1846, described the process:

The way the mules were broken to wagon harness would have astonished the "full-blooded" animals of Kentucky and other horse-raising states exceedingly. It is a treatment none but hardy Mexican or scrub mules could survive. They first had to be lassoed by our expert Mexican, Blas, their heads drawn up to a wagon wheel, with scarce two inches of spare rope to relax the tight noose on their necks and starved for twenty-four hours to subdue their fiery tempers; then harnessed to a heavy wagon, lashed unmercifully when they did not pull, whipped still harder when they ran at a still faster speed, until, after an hour's bewilderment and plunging and kicking, they became tractable and broken down—a labor-saving operation, with the unflinching motto of kill or cure.

Mules were easier to shoe, and their hoofs were so tough that they could even get along unshod, although their feet then became worn so smooth that they were likely to slip on steep hills. A "hee-haw minstrel," as wagoners sometimes called a mule, was tough and durable and relatively impervious to alkaline waters.

Mule skinners differed among themselves as to whether Mexican or Missouri mules were best. Actually the ancestors of the vaunted Missouri mules came mainly from Mexico. In 1823 traders brought 400 jacks, jennies, and mules from Santa Fe. When the donkeys were interbred with local horses, the Missouri mule was born. A few years later breeding animals were brought from the island of Malta to improve the stock.

If oxen were used to pull a wagon, it was customary to yoke six of them to the job. It took a ten-mule team to keep up with such an ox team.

A final innovation in high plains transport had

people in frontier Westport, Missouri—present-day Kansas City—scratching their heads in amazement. In antiquity the Chinese had built a windwagon, and an English inventor experimented with a vehicle propelled by paper kites, but none of this prepared the citizens of Westport for the seeming apparition that came sailing in off the plains one day in 1853.

Horses reared in fear, dogs yelped and ran for cover, and women whisked their children out of the way. It was "Windwagon Thomas" at the tiller of an odd vehicle that, propelled by a small sail, came rolling down the street. Thomas lowered the sail before Yoakum's Tavern, locked his brakes, and stepped indoors for a convivial drink. He announced that he was the "Navigator of the Prairies." He had come to enlist the town's aid in building a fleet of prairie clippers to carry cargo to Santa Fe.

The "Navigator of the Prairies" claimed the windwagon to be fast, economical, and free from the expense and delays of draft animals. The windwagon could leave the Arkansas River and sail across the prairies by compass, since there was no need to follow the river in order to find grazing and water for livestock. As for the Indians, they would be scared off at the sight of the strange vehicle.

After many convivial drinks the men in Yoakum's Tavern were still dubious, so Thomas announced that he would sail to Council Grove, about 150 miles away, and return so quickly that their reluctance would vanish on the wind. He went out, climbed into his windwagon, and sailed off down the street. Within nine days he was back from Council Grove with a letter from the blacksmith there as proof that he had actually made the trip.

The Westport men were convinced, and Dr. J. W. Parker, Henry Sager, Benjamin Newson, J. J. Mastin, and Thomas W. Adams joined Thomas in founding the Overland Navigation Company. They subscribed the funds to build the first wind-borne prairie schooner.

The wagon they built resembled a Conestoga rigged like a catboat. It was twenty-five feet long with a seven-foot beam. Its wheels were twelve feet in diameter, with hubs as huge as barrels. The cabin rose as far as the top of the wheels, and above that was the deck. The mast was stepped forward and carried a mainsail. The tailgate was in the bow, since the windwagon was designed to sail backwards with its tongue held up over the stern to serve as a tiller.

On the day of the windwagon's test, two yoke of oxen pulled it out onto the prairie. The founders of the Overland Navigation Company all clambered aboard except for Dr. Parker, who chose to follow the strange vehicle on a mule. The sail was hoisted, and the fresh wind caught hold. The vehicle went hurtling off, with Thomas at the tiller.

As they sped over the turf, the passengers cried for Thomas to shorten the sail and cut the speed, but he refused. All went well until he attempted to change direction. Then a gust of wind caught the sail, and the windwagon went into reverse. The doctor saw the wagon bearing down on him and dug his

heels into his mule's sides to urge it out of the way.

The helm locked, and the windwagon spun around and around in a mile-wide circle. Whenever it slowed a bit, one or more passengers leaped to the prairie for safety's sake. Thomas still refused to reef his sail. With a crash the windwagon lurched against a fence on the bank of Turkey Creek and was shipwrecked.

Windwagon Thomas did not have to be told that his colleagues of the Overland Navigation Company had no intention of repairing the vehicle. He got aboard his smaller windwagon and sailed off onto the prairies, never to be heard from again.

It was an ordeal for man and beast to shoe an ox, for oxen, unlike mules and horses, cannot stand on three legs. In some parts of the West the animal would be suspended from a sturdy frame in order to replace a shoe. In more primitive areas a shallow trench was dug. The ox was then turned upside down in it so that the blacksmith could get at the hoofs.

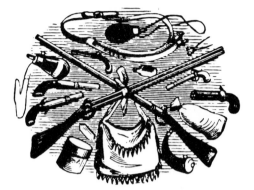

WITH THE MOUNTAIN MEN & EXPLORERS

ANYBODY COULD HEAR the trappers and their Red River carts coming for miles away across the northern high plains. Wooden wheels screamed on wooden axles. The only grease that the trappers could find to stop the screeching was pemmican, or sometimes the bodies of frogs, newts, and tadpoles captured in prairie ponds. The screech of their carts almost seemed to be a northern echo of the screech from the carretas of the Comancheros and the ciboleros far to the south.

The Red River cart was the invention of fur trader Alexander Henry, a field partner of the North West Company of Montreal. In 1801 he established a permanent post at Pembina, on the banks of the Red River of the North in what is today North Dakota. An incredible number of buffalo passed in herds within 100 feet of the fur traders' fort, and Henry's men could usually obtain a supply of meat simply by firing their guns from the gate. Even when the buffalo kept their distance from the post, an Indian called Le Boeuf had no trouble in bringing down all the game needed. A lean, gangling man, Le Boeuf was so fleet and so hardy that he could chase the buffalo on foot. He would run in the middle of the herd, loading and firing as he went, until he had killed as many buffalo as were required at the fort.

That same year Henry and his men made the first Red River cart in order to bring meat back to the fort from the site of the kill. The first cart had solid wheels sawed from the trunk of a tree, but the next year the trader built clumsy wheels with spokes that not only increased their strength but also lessened their weight.

In the decades to come the Red River carts spread out over the plains. They rolled as far west as Montana and as far south as Colorado, where their wheels screamed in earsplitting competition with those of the Spanish carretas. At the peak of the fur trade there were something like 8,000 Red River carts on the plains.

Henry and his men may have built the first of the carts, but it was the *métis*—half French, Scottish, or English, and half Indian—who made most of the thousands that followed. They fashioned the carts entirely of wood, without the use of nails or any other metal parts. The carts lumbered along on two large wheels, which the *métis* wrapped with buffalo rawhide because metal tires were unavailable in the wilderness. This method of lashing together the felloes was similar to that used thousands of years before on the wheels of Egyptian chariots. A block of oak made a hub, which was held in place by a wooden pin. Tired in rawhide, the wheels could pass over plashy prairie meadows better than metal-tired wheels could have done. A boxlike body rode high on the wooden axle so that the cart could be pulled through a stream without getting the cargo wet. Trappers spread a buffalo hide over the load to shelter it from the sun and the rain. If a river proved too deep to ford, the hide could be lashed tightly around the underside of the cart, thus turning it into a rude boat.

Above: *A half-breed bois brûlé, so called because they were said to be the color of burned wood, strikes a stance with his ox-drawn Red River cart at Pig's Eye on the upper Mississippi River in Minnesota. Pig's Eye later dropped its down-to-earth name in favor of Saint Paul and became the state's capital city.*

Right: *Wheels screamed as a string of Red River carts crossed the prairie. A minister preaching his sermon at a church in pioneer Saint Paul had no choice but to dismiss the congregation when the annual caravan of carts drew near. Everybody dashed outdoors to watch the métis arrive with their carts loaded with furs and hides.*

A cart might carry from 800 to 900 pounds of hides, furs, or pemmican, and it was usually pulled by a single ox, a mule, or a native range horse known as an Indian cayuse. One driver could handle from two to six carts. Each animal behind the lead animal would be tied by means of a rawhide strap to the rear of the cart ahead.

Jolly Joe Rolette was a *métis,* or a *bois brûlé,* so called because they were said to be the color of burned wood. In 1843 he led the first caravan of fur-laden carts through the Minnesota Valley to Saint Paul. *Bois brûlés* drove the 150 carts, each drawn by a single ox harnessed in shafts with strips of rawhide. They traveled about 15 miles a day and took about a month to reach Saint Paul from Pembina on the Red River, a distance of approximately 500 miles.

The settlers in Minnesota first saw a dense yellowish cloud of dust. It grew and grew as the carts came closer. Long before the men, oxen, and vehicles could be made out through the dust, the scream of the wheels had become torture. Settlers claimed that they could hear the carts coming from as far away as six miles. When the carts reached Saint Paul, on what came to be an annual journey, people listening to the din said, "Well, it's either a big fire or else Joe Rolette's in town."

The *métis* lived on both sides of the Canadian border. They farmed small plots of about fifteen acres, using their carts as farm wagons. Twice a year, in the middle of June and again in October, most of them would join together for a great buffalo hunt to the south, along the eastern flank of the Black Hills. They rendezvoused on the Pembina River;

elected a governor of the hunt, captains, guards, and guides; and adopted rules for the hunt to give everybody a fair share of the game. A Catholic priest usually went along to be sure that the rules were obeyed.

When everything was ready, the hunters set out with a guide, flaunting a flag at the head of the procession of carts. At night the *métis*—as a defense against the Sioux—arranged their carts in a circle with the shafts projecting out; the Indians took an increasingly dim view of their attacks on the buffalo herds. Pursuing and killing the cows because their meat was more tender, the *métis* wasted much of the carcasses. Men and women together cut the flesh into strips, as did the ciboleros to the south, and hung these on poles to dry in the sun, or dried them over a fire of buffalo chips. They rendered the fat in sheet-iron kettles and mixed it with dried meat to make pemmican. Bundles of pemmican and strips of jerked buffalo meat were loaded into the carts and brought back to Pembina or carried to Saint Paul, where they could be exchanged for sugar, coffee, and other supplies. Buffalo robes were also packed back to Pembina in the carts, for sale to fur traders.

So wasteful were the *métis* in their attacks on the buffalo that the U.S. Army as well as the Sioux took offense. In the summer of 1845 Capt. Edwin Sumner and a troop of dragoons from Fort Atkinson (Kansas) were in the field along with the Sioux to protect buffalo from the *métis*—one of the few times in the history of the northern plains when troopers and warriors found themselves on the same side in a campaign.

Métis, ciboleros, Comancheros, trappers and traders, and mountain men and explorers all played leapfrog across the West. Zebulon Montgomery Pike, Stephen H. Long, and Lt. James W. Abert discovered the tracks of Spanish carretas on the southern high plains when they thought they were in a trackless wilderness. The Red River carts reached the banks of the northern Missouri before Capt. Meriwether Lewis and William Clark ascended the river through what they believed to be unexplored territory. At least when an explorer moved into the high country on either side of the Continental Divide, he was not likely to discover that some enterprising unknown individual, usually of dusky complexion, had rolled a cart down the trail ahead of him.

In 1812, when Robert Stuart and his small party of Astorians trekked eastward from the coast of Oregon through South Pass in Wyoming and on to Saint Louis, he saw nothing of wheeled vehicles. But he thought of wagons as he made the long, arduous journey. He reached Saint Louis on April 30, 1813. On May 15 the *Missouri Gazette* reported: "By information received from these gentlemen,

it appears that a journey across the continent of North America might be performed with a wagon, there being no obstruction on the whole route that any person would dare to call a mountain in addition to its being much the most direct and short one to go from this place to the mouth of the Columbia River."

Only the future would tell. Twelve years passed before Jedediah Strong Smith, the mountain man who carried the Bible and a copy of Shakespeare's plays in his pack, crossed the Great Divide moving from east to west, and seven more years went by before mountain men traversed the entire length of what was to be known as the Oregon Trail. Like Stuart, Smith was convinced that wagons could go where he had walked. Not until 1830 was a wagon hauled from the Missouri frontier all the way to a tributary of the Columbia River.

William Henry Ashley, brigadier general in the Missouri militia and fur trader extraordinary, employed some 300 men in the West. Mountain men in Ashley's service followed the route of the Oregon Trail to the Rockies, and Ashley was familiar with the successful use of wagon trains on the trail to Santa Fe. When his trappers assembled with pack mules and horses at Fort Atkinson (Nebraska) late in October, 1824, in preparation for a journey to the Rockies, he decided to send along a single wagon as an experiment. Wagons, he reasoned, do not have to be packed and unpacked every day as mules do. True enough, a pack train could travel faster and go through rougher country, but a wagon train would require fewer men and animals. Thus the first wheeled vehicle to start over the Oregon Trail rolled westward. The November blizzards were severe that year, and somewhere along the Loup Fork in east central Nebraska the snow became so deep that the wagon had to be abandoned.

The failure of his wagon to get through the drifts discouraged Ashley, but when he left Saint Louis in March, 1826, on his way to a trappers' rendezvous at Great Salt Lake, he trundled along a four-pounder cannon on a crude carriage drawn by two mules. Ashley and his men managed to get the cannon through South Pass and down through a tumble of rugged mountains to Great Salt Lake. The cannon became the first wheeled vehicle to cross the Continental Divide on the Oregon Trail. It created a furor when Ashley demonstrated its prowess before the mountain men and Indians at the rendezvous. When word got out that he had succeeded in drawing a cannon on wheels through South Pass, it created

quite a stir along the frontier too. Where the cannon had rolled, a wagon could roll.

Smith and David E. Jackson were partners with William L. Sublette, an adventurous Virginian, in what later became the Rocky Mountain Fur Company. Sublette was half convinced by Smith's certainty that a wagon could be pulled over the mountains, and Ashley's cannon convinced him the rest of the way. On April 10, 1830, Sublette and a party of eighty-one men started back for the Rockies with twelve wheeled vehicles. Ten of them were high-sided Murphy wagons built in Saint Louis for the Santa Fe Trail trade. Each Murphy wagon carried 1,800 pounds of trading goods and was drawn by five mules. Sublette observed that with the wagons twenty-two men and fifty-two mules could carry as much freight as forty-five men and a pack train of ninety mules could carry. Sublette also brought along two light four-wheeled carriages called dearborns, a type of vehicle first introduced into the West by the U.S. Army and named for Henry Dearborn, secretary of war under Thomas Jefferson. The dearborns had curtains on the sides, and Sublette used the carriages to carry himself and his belongings. Each dearborn was pulled by a single mule.

As Sublette's party crossed the plains, road builders ranged ahead to cut down the banks of ravines along river courses so that the wagons could cross the streams. The men even built a crude bridge across Cannonball Creek in Kansas. The wagon train —the first to go over the Platte River stretch of the Oregon Trail—entered Wyoming near Scottsbluff, Nebraska, and continued to the Wind River Rendezvous. It reached its destination on July 16, and the rendezvous erupted into a binge fueled by quantities of diluted grain alcohol.

Sublette left the two dearborns in the mountains, where they were a curiosity for a while to the Indians and mountain men. Loading the Murphy wagons with fur, he yoked up a single milk cow and the beef cattle that had survived the rendezvous and hauled them back to civilization.

Newspapers not only in Saint Louis but also in the East vied with one another in praising the exploit. Sublette had shown the way to take wagons through the mountains. Wheels could roll west. As for Sublette, he went back to the use of pack mules for his next several trips. When people asked why, he explained laconically that on the high plains and in the mountains there was no place to reforge an iron tire or recaulk the leaky seams of a wagon box. Doubters observed that Sublette's wagons had

Above: *Fort Laramie on the Oregon Trail began as a fur traders' stockade in 1834 and was strengthened until it became the bastion of the trail. From Fort Laramie troopers rode out to aid beleaguered wagon trains or to help besieged forts. It was also the social center of Wyoming Territory. Lieutenant Caspar Collins wrote to his mother: "They make the soldiers wear white gloves at this post, and they cut around very fashionably." Pioneer wives put on gloves to ride into the fort too, although their gloves may have been soiled from picking up buffalo chips for the campfires.*

Below: *Nathaniel Wyeth, a Massachusetts ice cutter who built three huge amphibious freight wagons shaped like boats, founded Fort Hall in 1834. Two years later he sold it to the Hudson's Bay Company. The British flag welcomed American wagons to the fort, although it was on American territory. Fort Hall was the only outpost in hundreds of miles where the traveler could be assured of frontier hospitality.*

not crossed the Continental Divide. There still would be a great deal of trouble ahead before wheels could roll through to the Pacific.

It was a U.S. Army captain who first took wagons across the Continental Divide. Capt. Benjamin Louis Eulalie de Bonneville of the Seventh Infantry was as French-born as his name suggests, but he was a graduate of West Point. Although the stocky Bonneville was scarcely the rangy frontiersman of legend and story, he was strong and vigorous; in 1831, at the age of thirty-five, he was prematurely bald. Above all he had an inquiring mind, which caused him to ask General Macomb, his commanding officer, for a leave of absence from the Army on May 21, 1831, presumably to explore and map unknown parts of the West. Whether this was his true intention is still a matter of controversy. Certainly he appears to have had a desire to set himself up in the lucrative fur trade as well.

Bonneville also owed a debt to the experiences of wagon masters on the Santa Fe Trail. Joseph Reddeford Walker, a veteran of the Santa Fe trade, offered to accompany him over the Oregon Trail. Bonneville and Walker agreed with Sublette that wagons could save time for a party traveling into the West. They would not have to be unloaded every night and reloaded in the morning, as pack animals must be. There would be trouble in getting them through streams and through badlands, but wagons could also be formed into a mobile fort in case of Indian attack.

Bonneville's wagons were scarcely the huge Conestoga, Pittsburgh, or Murphy wagons used to haul freight to Santa Fe. They were even smaller than the emigrants' wagons that were to follow in their trail some ten years later. They also had wooden axles. Iron axles were already known on the trail to Santa Fe, but iron sometimes snapped under the punishment of the high plains. Then the entire wagon had to be abandoned. A wooden axle could be replaced in some fashion or other, and the wagon could continue its journey.

On May 1, 1832, Bonneville and Walker set out from Fort Osage on the Missouri River, close to the present town of Sibley, Missouri. The expedition consisted of 110 men and twenty wagons drawn by mules and oxen. By May 13 the party was some 100 miles out on the trail. Bonneville built rafts to float his wagons across the Kansas River, which the spring floods had sent out of its banks. Later he crossed other rivers, such as the South Platte and the Laramie, by taking off the wheels and sheathing the wagon boxes in hides to make them into bullboats. Bonneville reported that in crossing the Platte he "caused the bodies of the wagons to be dislodged from the wheels, covered them with buffalo hides, besmeared with a compound of tallow and ashes, thus forming rude boats."

The men corduroyed soft spots in the trail with saplings that they had cut along the riverbanks and hacked dugouts, or half-roads, through steep banks. Bonneville reported in a letter to General Macomb that he frequently resorted to "letting [his] wagons down the bluffs with long ropes, eighty men to each wagon."

Bluffs and river crossings were dangerous and troublesome, but it was the dry air of the high plains that caused the most trouble. Washington Irving, who wrote a best-selling book—*The Adventures of Captain Bonneville*—upon the captain's return to civilization, explained, "The woodwork of the wagons also shrank so much that it was with difficulty the wheels were kept from falling to pieces."

Spokes, hubs, and felloes shrank from the dryness, so that iron tires fell off and had to be replaced. First wedges were used. On the Sweetwater River Bonneville's men removed the tire from each wheel and whittled out flexible arcs of wood, which were nailed to the outside of the felloe, or rim. They placed the tires in hot flames until they glowed red, slipped them into place on the felloes, and then dipped them into cold water to make them tight. When they ran out of nails, the men learned to use rawhide cords to bind the wood together. They also learned that they could take the disintegrating wheels off their wagons and submerge them in creeks overnight to swell them back to normal.

Bonneville followed the trail blazed by Sublette as far as he could. When he came to the eastern slope of the Rockies, he went up the Sweetwater River and through South Pass, which he crossed on July 24. He was the first person to take wagons through South Pass. It seemed anticlimactic as the wagons rolled through the broad, gentle pass, where the backbone of the continent is imperceptible. Rolling on to the banks of the Green River, he built Fort Bonneville at a place that knowledgeable mountain men found laughable. They knew that he had selected a spot where snows pile up every winter to incredible depths. That winter one storm after another completely buried the sturdy little wagons that had become the first to cross the Continental Divide. They had done their job, and they were left beside the fort to decay.

BREAKING UP CAMP AT SUNRISE by Alfred Jacob Miller
WALTERS ART GALLERY

SANTA FE TRADERS by Frank Tenney Johnson
EXCHANGE BANK & TRUST COMPANY, DALLAS

ATTACK ON THE SUPPLY TRAIN by Frederic Remington
DR. HAROLD MC CRACKEN

RED RIVER CART by William Cary

Americans have always shown an inventive turn of mind when it comes to transportation. Among the vehicles to roll west in the years to come were some strange and wonderful creations—the wind-wagon, the steam wagon, and a whole fleet of other contraptions. The first extraordinary vehicle intended for use in the West was the masterwork of a Massachusetts ice cutter. Nathaniel Jarvis Wyeth cut ice on a pond near Boston and shipped it to New Orleans and the West Indies at a good profit. Hauling ice to the Boston docks made him think of wagons, and reading about the challenge of taking a wagon across the continent made him think of what kind of wagon might be most suitable in the West. At last he constructed three huge freight wagons, thirteen feet long and four feet wide, that were shaped like boats. The joints were dovetailed so perfectly that they were watertight even without an application of oakum. All a wagoner had to do was disengage the wheels, and the wagon became a boat ready to cross a wilderness river.

As Wyeth and his friends drove the wagons through 'the streets of Cambridge, a crowd jeered. Kids chased after the lumbering amphibians, which everybody on hand for the fun dubbed "Nat-wye-thums." Hoping to reach the Far West, Wyeth managed to get his wagon-boats as far as Saint Louis. Kenneth McKenzie of the American Fur Company looked over the "Nat-wye-thums" and said that they would be too heavy to pull through the demonic terrain over which Wyeth must travel, and would be likely to turn turtle in a mountain stream's fast water. Dejectedly, Wyeth sold the wagons for half their cost, and on May 13, 1832, started west from Independence with William Sublette along the route taken by Bonneville just about two weeks before.

Where Bonneville and Sublette had taken wagons, other fur traders drove wagons too. At least they now took vehicles in increasing numbers as far as Fort Laramie in Wyoming. Lucien Fontenelle of the American Fur Company was one of the most enterprising of the traders. In 1835 he brought six light wagons, pack stock, and more than sixty men on a trip to Fort Laramie, where he intended to trade for buffalo robes. By then the trip with wagons was routine, except that Fontenelle's brigade had a pair of odd guests. They were the Reverend Samuel Parker, a preposterous figure on the plains in his schoolmaster's coat and plug hat, and missionary doctor Marcus Whitman, a pious man with stubborn blue eyes and a determined mouth. The first night on the trail the mountain men got drunk and pelted the two Presbyterians with rotten eggs.

Whitman pitched in and helped the men to build crude bridges so that the wagons and mules could cross tributary streams along the Missouri River. He treated a cholera epidemic that struck in eastern Nebraska, and he studied the wagons. To the men of Fontenelle's brigade the wagons were a means to wealth. To Whitman they meant the settlement of Oregon, for he was already determined to open up the vast Northwest to American families. Only wagons could take families and their belongings to the land beyond the mountains.

Jim Beckwourth, mountain man and self-styled Indian chief, was the son of a white plantation owner and his mulatto slave. Jim knew the high mountains and led wagon trains through them to the Far West, where he settled in California. Later he moved to Denver.

In his *Journal of an Exploring Tour beyond the Rocky Mountains*, the Reverend Parker described the way the brigade camped at night:

The manner of our encamping, is to form a large hollow square, encompassing an area of about an acre, having the river on one side; three wagons forming a part of another side, coming down to the river; and three more in the same manner on the opposite side; and the packages so arranged in parcels, about three rods apart, as to fill up the rear, and the sides not occupied by the wagons. The horses and mules, near the middle of the day, are turned out under guard, to feed for two hours; and the same again towards night, until after sunset, when they are taken up and brought into the hollow square, and fastened with ropes twelve feet long, to pickets driven firmly into the ground.

Men wrapped themselves in their blankets to sleep, sometimes under the wagons, sometimes under the stars. They kept guard at night, relieving the guard every two hours.

Fontenelle, like Bonneville, forded rivers by removing the wheels from his wagons and covering the wagons with skins, and he too had a laborious time getting his wagons through. He took them only as far as Fort Laramie. He pushed on with pack stock to the Green River Rendezvous of 1835, and Whitman and Parker went with him. Mountain men from all over the wilderness had come together to drink, dance, gamble, lust after the Indian women, race their horses, and quarrel, which was the most fun of all. When drunken trappers seized Whitman and tried to force a bottle of whiskey into his mouth, he clenched his teeth and furiously said that they could hold his head under water, but he would never let a swallow of the wicked fluid pass his throat.

More important, Whitman also dug a three-year-old Blackfoot arrowhead out of Jim Bridger's back as Jim, fortified by a huge pull at a whiskey bottle as an anesthetic, bit on a piece of wood. Whitman spent the rest of the rendezvous digging old bullets and arrowheads out of the tough hides of mountain men. As he dug with his scalpel, he learned from the mountain men about the land beyond the Green River. Could he get a wagon through it?

The wedding of Narcissa Prentiss and Marcus Whitman took place at the Presbyterian church at Angelica, New York, as soon as the doctor returned from the West to persuade the Board of Missions to send more missionaries. Narcissa appeared in the church door in a wedding dress of black bombazine, already in love not only with the doctor but also with his dreams of saving Indian souls and opening a way for wagon wheels to roll to Oregon. The bridegroom symbolically entered with an Indian boy whom he

had brought back with him. The boy from the savage West stood at his elbow during the ceremony to remind everybody that Narcissa was marrying not only a man, but his dream.

Whitman told the Board of Missions that he would save bodies and souls among the Indians and find a way for wagons to reach Oregon. Then he set out with his auburn-haired bride.

The Board of Missions had decided to send not one missionary couple, but two, into the mountains. The Reverend Henry Harmon Spalding and his wife Eliza were chosen as the second couple. When he heard where his daughter was going, Eliza Spalding's father presented her with a horse, a harness, and a dearborn wagon specially constructed out of seasoned woods for western roads. The Spaldings attached sleigh runners to the wagon and set out in the winter for Cincinnati, where they boarded a riverboat bound for Saint Louis. They shipped the wagon on the boat deck, but they sold the horse.

The missionary party outfitted at Liberty, Missouri, where they bought fourteen horses and six

Above: *Sir William Drummond Stewart, a British nobleman who preferred life on the American frontier to life on his estate, brought two carts with him on a trip into the Rockies. He abandoned them at Fort Laramie. His arrival at the foot of the Wind River Mountains, Wyoming, in 1843, was painted by Alfred Jacob Miller, an artist member of his expedition.*

Left: *Jim Bridger, one of the great scouts of the western frontier, could see that the rough-and-tumble days of the mountain men were drawing to a close. In 1864 Jim established a ferry to help wagon trains cross the North Platte River, close to present-day Orin, Wyoming, but he still guided an occasional train through the wild country that he had come to know so well.*

mules to pull Eliza's wagon and a heavy farm wagon purchased by the Whitmans. William H. Gray, another medical missionary, joined the party and helped to drive the wagons. Later, out on the plains, Whitman picked up a teenaged boy named Miles Goodyear, who was making his lonely way west, and out of compassion added him to the party. Scouting ahead on a horse, the boy was in his glory.

On the plains the group also caught up with Thomas Fitzpatrick, a mountain man renowned throughout the West as "Broken Hand," who was leading a company of trappers and seven big freight wagons, each drawn by six mules. When Sir William Stewart, one of the incredible British noblemen who preferred roughing it on the American frontier to life in settled Britain, came along with two more carts, the combined party made quite an impressive wagon train as it strung out across the prairie.

At Fort Laramie Fitzpatrick and Stewart alike left their vehicles, and Fitzpatrick urged Whitman to do the same. The doctor gave up the heavy farm wagon, but he took the dearborn wagon with him. Eliza Spalding was ailing, and he explained to Fitzpatrick that she could ride in the dearborn. He loaded as many of the supplies in the wagon as it would hold, and the company set off for the Green River Rendezvous.

Journeying over the rough trail beyond Fort Laramie, the missionaries and their wives fell far behind the mountain men. Their wagon upset as often as four and five times a day. Even though Fitzpatrick sent two trappers back to help the missionaries with their wagon, they ended up so far behind each day that Whitman had to drive after dark to reach the camp.

Chopping cottonwood logs to help the wagon cross marshy bottomlands, digging through gully banks, leveling off hillsides so that the wagon could pass, the Whitman party struggled through the wilderness. They stopped at Independence Rock and became the first people to write their names on the rock with axle grease. Long after the names carved in the rock had vanished, the names written with grease remained.

At the rendezvous friendly Indians and trappers alike insisted that Whitman should not try to take the wagon farther. Bonneville had given up at the Green River, and the mountains that lay ahead were much too precipitous and tangled for a wagon. But Whitman was adamant. In his imagination he could see the wagon trains of the future making their way over a trail through the mountains, and he would not leave the wagon behind.

The missionary party and their wagon pushed farther west. The wagon upset again and again on the steep hillsides. Narcissa Whitman wrote in her journal, "It was a greater wonder that it was not turning somersaults continually."

When the vehicle mired in a creek, Whitman struggled waist-deep in the icy water to get it loose. Finally, a week after leaving the rendezvous, an axle broke beneath the heavy load. "They are making a cart of the hind wheels this afternoon and lashing the forward wheels to it, intending to take it through in some shape or another," Narcissa jotted in her journal.

Whitman worked into the night by lamplight to finish the job. In the morning the wagon, now cut down to a cart, was hitched to the mules. Whitman had tied the front wheels onto the cart, so that he could reassemble the vehicle once he had passed the mountains. At last the party reached Fort Hall.

Goodyear had bruised his shoulders once too often while helping to push the vehicle out of a mudhole or over a river crossing. Unless the doctor gave up the wagon, Goodyear was not going any farther. There was still no question, however, in the stubborn doctor's mind. The wagon must go through to Oregon. Seeing that he could not shake Whitman's resolve, the boy heaved a sigh and went off with a party of fur trappers. Later he made his way to California, where, in the summer of 1849, he settled at what was to be known as Goodyear's Bar, where Goodyear's Creek joins the North Yuba River in the middle of the goldfields.

On August 4 the missionaries left Fort Hall. Whitman had removed the box from the cart, but he still insisted on continuing with the running gear. Joseph L. Meek, a tough old mountain man, took a look at the odd contraption bouncing along the mountainside. "Thar goes the fur trade," he is reported to have said. "When wheels kin cross the Rockies, then comes the settlers."

Somehow Whitman got to a ford through the Boise River. There the wagon turned upside down in the rushing torrent. The mules tangled in the harness and almost drowned. The men put two of their horses to the cart and swam one horse on either side of it to get it across.

It was not far to Fort Boise. There Rotten Belly, a Nez Percé chief, took pity on the doctor, who he thought must be crazy. He offered to take off the iron tires and flatten them out, so that they could be packed on horses and taken farther west. He could not understand why his solution to the problem left the now angry doctor more apoplectic than ever. At last there was nothing to do but leave what remained of the wagon at Fort Boise. For years afterwards the remains were pointed out to greenhorns as one of the wonders of the West. Mountain men could not stop talking about the incredible contraption that the mad doctor had brought all the way to Fort Boise.

Narcissa and Marcus Whitman continued to a point on the Walla Walla River that was only twenty miles from the Hudson's Bay Company's Fort Walla Walla. Cayuse tribesmen helped the doctor to build a log mission, known as Waiilatpu, that was to be one of the landmarks of the trail to Oregon. Whitman could rightly claim that he had brought wheels through the mountains to a tributary of the Columbia. And Narcissa Whitman and Eliza Spalding could claim that they were the first white women to reach Oregon.

Above: *In 1845 the Whitman Mission at Waiilatpu was a hospitable stop at the far end of the Oregon Trail. Then the 1847 emigrant train brought measles to the mission. The epidemic spread to the nearby Cayuse village, where many died. Marcus Whitman, true to his calling as a physician, did what he could to save the lives of the suffering Indians. Angered by his failure, the Indians killed both him and his wife and destroyed the mission.*

Below: *Situated eight miles below the point where the Boise River flows into the Snake, the Hudson's Bay Company's Fort Boise was an important landmark on the Oregon Trail. There Rotten Belly, a Nez Percé chief, took pity on Whitman. Fanatically fighting to get a wagon over the mountains, Whitman had reached Fort Boise with his wagon falling to pieces. Rotten Belly offered to remove the iron tires from the wheels and flatten them, so that they could be packed on horses and taken farther west. The kind suggestion made the doctor apoplectic, but there was nothing for him to do but leave the wagon at the fort. For years afterwards mountain men pointed it out as the incredible contraption that the mad doctor had managed to bring all the way to Fort Boise.*

One day in 1840 Whitman received a very happy surprise. Meek and two other fur trappers, Robert Newell and Caleb Wilkins, had taken the running gears of three wagons abandoned at Fort Hall through the Blue Mountains to Waiilatpu. They had rolled the wheels west behind Indian ponies. It was now time for Whitman, who had astounded Meek, to be in turn astonished as well as delighted.

According to James Hewitt in his *Eye-Witnesses to Wagon Trains West*, Whitman cried, "You have broken the ice, and when others see that wagons have passed, they, too, will pass, and in a few years the valley will be full of our people."

The running gears stayed at Whitman's mission over the winter. Indian mothers and their children took rides on them, while their dark eyes sparkled with the wonder and pleasure of it. The next spring Newell, better known in the mountains as "Doc," came back; loading the wheels onto a barge, he floated them down the Columbia River to the Willamette. From there it would be just a short roll, downhill all the way, to the pounding surf on the ocean beaches.

In the fall of 1842 Whitman left Oregon to journey to Washington, D.C., where he testified before a congressional committee about the need for legislation to help people emigrating to Oregon. A senator heatedly charged that there was no road.

"You are mistaken, sir!" fired back Whitman. "There is a road, and I made it. I've taken wheels all the way to Oregon."

It was during the same year, 1842, that John Charles Frémont received a commission from Lt. Col. John James Abert, chief of the U.S. Corps of Topographical Engineers, to explore the road to Oregon as far as the Wind River Mountains in western Wyoming. The U.S. government was now bent on scientifically examining a territory already well explored in other respects. Frémont loaded his supplies, scientific instruments, and an India-rubber boat onto eight carts, and in late spring he headed out onto the plains. Shortly after leaving Saint Louis, he encountered western scout Kit Carson, who offered to accompany him as a guide. Frémont accepted Carson's offer, and the two men became lifelong friends.

On June 14 he unlimbered his rubber boat, which was twenty feet long and five feet broad. He wheeled a cart aboard the boat and ferried it across the Kansas River. Growing impatient with the slow process of ferrying one cart across the river at a time, Frémont ordered that the two remaining carts be put on the boat together. The boat slipped out to midstream and then upset beneath the weight. This proved disastrous as far as a Frenchman on the expedition was concerned. One of the two carts drenched in the river contained most of their coffee. Who could continue on a trip into the savage wilderness without coffee?

On July 28, 1842, near Fort Laramie in Wyoming, Frémont dismantled his carts and hid them among the willows on the banks of the Platte. He had no faith in wheels climbing over the Continental Divide, particularly when Indians warned him that a severe drought and a plague of grasshoppers ahead had destroyed the grass needed for his draft animals. On August 26 Frémont returned from his trip through South Pass, retrieved the carts, and returned to Bellevue on the Missouri, where he sold them at auction.

Frémont made another trip with a wheeled vehicle into the West in 1843. This time it was a howitzer that he brought from Saint Louis to the Sierra Nevadas of California. There he was forced by the seemingly impassable mountains to abandon the howitzer, although he noted, "It was of the kind invented by the French for the mountain part of their war in Algiers; and the distance it had come with us proved how well it was adapted to its purpose."

Frémont's failure to get his howitzer through the Sierra Nevadas made it seem unlikely that wheels would be rolling into California for some time to come, but wagon trains of settlers were already striking out for Oregon over the trails pioneered by Whitman. As they rolled across the high plains, they encountered wagons coming east from Fort Laramie loaded with buffalo hides. These wagons were driven by mountain men, rough-hewn, bearded, and long-haired, wearing hunting shirts and moccasins of deerskin.

The mountain men stared at the women and children riding the wagons west. Meek had been right. The wheels had crossed the Rockies, and here came the settlers. The fur trade was bound to perish, and their way of life was coming to an end.

ALONG THE EMIGRANT TRAILS

IT WAS SEPTEMBER 1976. My wife Joan and I had come to Little Eagle, a Hunkpapa Sioux village on the Standing Rock Indian Reservation of north central South Dakota, in a car with four-wheel drive, but now a train of four authentic covered wagons was ready to roll. The drivers had caught up their teams, and the wagons had fallen into line.

"Move out! Move out!" shouted wagon master Maynard Sogge.

With a jolting and rumbling of the iron-tired wheels, a jingling and jangling of harness, and a clopping of horses' hoofs on high prairie turf, the wagons were off. Joan rode shotgun beside the driver of one of the wagons, and I was flopped in the tail of the wagon, where I tossed and bumped with each turn of the springless wheel. No wonder that wagon train families used to hang pails of cream onto the rear axle to let the jolting churn the cream into butter. We lurched out into the grassy hills. In a few minutes the few houses of the village were gone, and the turning wheels had taken us back into the nineteenth century, when wagons were the way people traveled to new homes beyond the sunset.

Sogge first took a wagon train through the range country from Mobridge, on the Missouri River, to Deadwood for the annual "Days of '76" celebration some eight years ago. Now he takes vacationers from all over the country on summer wagon train rides. Judging from the similar ratio of people to wagons on actual emigrant trains, four wagons were plenty for our party of fifteen tenderfeet and a crew of sev-

en: four drivers, a trail master, a scout, and a cook.

In the old days such a small train might have run into trouble from the Indians. We would have had nothing to worry about, however, because our drivers were Hunkpapa, and Sogge is married to a Hunkpapa woman. The two lively boys sporting around the wagons as we bumped down the trail were Indian lads, and so was the seventeen-year-old scout surveying the land ahead.

The horses and wagons threw up dust on the dry prairie. Even so, it was pleasurable to employ "ankle express," as the pioneers called walking. This was particularly true if a hiker fell lazily to the rear, where the serenity of the high plains was a balm for the twentieth-century spirit. Sharp-tailed grouse whirred up, and prairie falcons wheeled overhead. Antelope sped along the distant hills, and once we scared one up in a river break. It sprinted through the brush. We passed through a prairie dog village. We camped at night under the western stars within the sheltering circle of our wagons, and we told tall tales and listened to the coyotes yelping.

We fell heir to a problem common among old-time wagon trains. Felloes, shrinking in the dry air, separated from the iron tires, and we had to stop and drive wedges beneath the iron to tighten the wheels. Spokes broke. The wagon master ordered that a wagon wheel be soaked in a river overnight to swell the wood again.

One morning the draft horses spooked and ran off into the hills, and it took several hours search-

Above: *Wagon master Maynard Sogge guides his twentieth-century wagon train over the high plains of South Dakota. The wagons bounce and rumble over ranch roads and prairie turf. The turning wheels take present-day Americans back into the nineteenth century, when wagons like this one carried settlers to new homes in the West.*

Left: *Sogge's wagon train falls heir to the same misadventures that plagued the westering emigrant trains of yesteryear. In the arid atmosphere the felloes of the wheels shrink and separate from the iron tires. The party has to stop from time to time and drive wedges beneath the iron to tighten the wheels. At night one of the wagon wheels has to be soaked in a river to swell the wood again.*

Below: *Horses on the contemporary Dakota wagon train ran off into the hills and had to be rounded up by men on horseback. One horse jerked at the wagon to which it had been tied until it yanked the box right off the running gear. The men of the party picked up the box and placed it back on the gear, where it could be fastened into place once more.*

ing on horseback to round them up; and another horse, which showed the disposition of a mule, jerked at the wagon to which it had been tied, until it had yanked the box right off the running gear. We fastened the box neatly into place once more.

We rough-locked down steep hills and forded the Grand River. On the last day of our journey, we came upon a party of Indians stuck with their pickup truck in the soft river sands. As we wagon train people pushed the truck to firm ground, we couldn't help but feel that the old ways of travel on the High Plains were proving better than the new, at least for the moment. At the same time we had a firsthand appreciation of the problems and hardships of frontier transportation.

The wheels that carried the pioneers into the West came in all sizes and kinds. There were the wheels of Conestoga wagons, common lumber wagons used on farms, handcarts, Murphy wagons, buggies, and even wheelbarrows. In 1850 a Scotsman arrived at Fort Laramie pushing a wheelbarrow loaded with his gear. He continued as far as the Great Salt Lake, where he abandoned his one-wheel transport. A. O. McGrew, a printer from Pennsylvania, trundled a wheelbarrow loaded with clothing, food, and mining tools from the Missouri River to the Colorado goldfields in 1859. Later he returned to the East to become city editor of the *New York Evening News*.

At first very few Conestoga wagons made the trip, because the trails were rough and difficult for any vehicle as heavy and big as those redoubtable freight wagons. They were more at home in the East and on the Santa Fe Trail. Then, as railroads spread through the eastern states into the Midwest in the 1850s, Conestogas were no longer needed in large numbers on eastern roads. They were loaded on riverboats and taken to the frontier, where pioneers bought them at bargain prices to carry their families west. By then the trails had become rough roads, and the wagons could get through. At no time did the Conestoga dominate the western emigrant trails.

Randolph Barnes Marcy, who spent much of his life on the plains, advised emigrants as to the right wagons for the trip west in *The Prairie Traveler*, which he wrote as a handbook for emigrants at the request of the War Department:

Wagons should be of the simplest possible construction—strong, light, and made of well-seasoned timber, especially the wheels, as the atmosphere, in the elevated and arid region over which they have to pass, is so exceedingly dry during the summer months that, unless the wood-work is thoroughly seasoned, they will require constant repairs to prevent them from falling to pieces.

Wheels made of the bois-d'arc, or Osage orange-wood, are the best for the plains, as they shrink but little, and seldom want repairing. As, however, this wood is not easily procured in the Northern States, white oak answers a very good purpose if well seasoned. . . .

The pole of the wagon should have a joint where it enters the hounds, to prevent the weight from coming upon it and breaking the hounds in passing short and abrupt holes in the road.

The perch or coupling-pole should be shifting or movable, as, in the event of the loss of a wheel, an axle, or other accident rendering it necessary to abandon the wagon, a temporary cart may be constructed out of the remaining portion. The tires should be examined just before commencing the journey, and, if not perfectly snug, reset.

One of the chief causes of accidents to carriages upon the plains arises from the nuts coming off from the numerous bolts that secure the running gearing. To prevent this, the ends of all the bolts should be riveted; it is seldom necessary to take them off, and when this is required the ends of the bolts may easily be filed away.

For the most part emigrants used farm wagons made by country blacksmiths. In 1853 John Studebaker, later to join his brothers in making the famed Studebaker wagons, built a wagon with the help of one of his brothers and started west in it. Unlike the Conestoga and Murphy wagons, the covered wagons of the emigrants usually had straight beds. They had what Chester Ingersoll, a pioneer at Independence in 1849, called "the Ohio form," with wide tracks and boxes two feet high and eleven feet long. Ingersoll, who was from northern Illinois, claimed that wagons made in his home section were best, but then he also claimed that the oxen from northern Illinois were the fastest.

Another type of vehicle favored by emigrants was called the New England wagon for the part of the country where it was built. It too lacked the Conestoga's undercurve. It had straight sides that were long and low, and both its sides and its ends flared out to provide more space. Characteristically it carried a water barrel on one side of the bed and a long toolbox on the other.

Some emigrant wagons were made in the West. In New Braunfels, Texas, on the Old San Antonio Road, German settlers proved to be superb wagonmakers as early as the 1840s. They made large and rugged wagons pulled by three to four span of mules or five to six yoke of oxen, each with a brass bell jingling around its neck. The 1850 U.S. Census shows six wagonmakers, twelve cartwrights, and one wheelwright in the frontier town. All are described as natives of Germany. The house of the first Ger-

man wagonmaker in New Braunfels may still be seen on Mill Street.

Sometimes a false bottom was built into the wagon box to hold valuables. Plainsman J. M. Shively suggested that the wagon bed be lined with "wooden boxes of half or three-fourth inch pine boards, to put provisions." Closed by hinges, the boxes would make comfortable chairs for women and children to sit on during the day, and beds to sleep on at night. Helen M. Carpenter, another pioneer, had a double-deck arrangement in her wagon, with the supplies and provisions on the floor and the bedding above.

The bows of the typical pioneer wagon were rounded, but Helen Carpenter's rig had square bows to provide her family with extra headroom. Many pioneer families sewed pockets on the inside of the canvas covering and kept useful things handy in them. As for the covering itself, it might be of osnaburg duck—named for Osnabrück, Germany, where it was first made—rainproof canvas, well-oiled or painted linen, white drilling, muslin, sailcloth, or oilcloth. Some of the best coverings were made by a sailmaker who had emigrated to Saint Louis from the East Coast and set up shop in the Old Rock House on the riverfront, where pelts were stored during the heyday of the fur traders.

Nor were all the coverings white. They were sometimes painted blue, green, or red, and the emigrants often enlivened them with slogans such as "Pikes Peak or Bust," or "Californy, Here We Come!" Another popular phrase was "Fifty-four Forty or Fight!" These slogans reflected the emigrants' chosen destinations, but others were selected

Above: *The Colorado Gold Rush pioneers scrawled "Pikes Peak or Bust" on their wagon tops and started across the plains to the goldfields. Many of the gold seekers "busted" and returned home poorer in pocket than when they started, but richer in experience.*

Left, top: *The interior of a covered wagon contained much that was dear to a pioneer family. Often, as the trails grew more difficult and the draft animals weakened, the choicest possessions had to be set out by the side of the road to be taken by anyone who happened along.*

Left, bottom: *An indomitable wagon train family stares into a pioneer camera set up on the high plains. To leave behind a familiar world in the East and go journeying into the West in search of a better life called for the determination and strength of character manifest in this early photograph. The wagon tongues made appropriate seats for anyone who wanted to rest for a bit.*

for different reasons. One man painted "I'll Get There" on his tarpaulin, together with an imaginative landscape of a peak piercing some clouds. A family whose prairie schooner was drawn by six milk cows emblazoned their covering with "Family Express—Milk for Sale," and a party of misanthropes enhanced theirs with "The Eleventh Commandment—Mind Your Own Business." Seeing the first buffalo herds on the plains was one of the great adventures for the emigrants, and pioneers often wrote the date of their first sighting of buffalo on their wagon boxes.

A great variety of vehicles followed the trails west. Between the Missouri River and Cherry Creek, Colorado, one traveler saw wagons, buggies, sulkies, wheelbarrows, and handcarts. One outfit even had a small cart drawn by a team of dogs. The museum at Ogallala, Nebraska, contains a goat harness. It belonged to a team of goats that pulled a cart west along the Mormon Trail. One family went west in Red River carts. John W. Jones and his party were en route from Faribault, Minnesota, to Oregon in July, 1858, when, according to his manuscript journal in the Newberry Library in Chicago, they overtook "a Red River team, homeward bound. They were camped near a lake, waiting for reinforcements as they were afraid of the predatory bands of Sioux who infested that portion of the country, and who would not spare a team that came in their way if numerically stronger. The train was comprised of half-breeds with Red River carts, a curiosity, by the way, being destitute of iron with the exceptions of the staples in the shafts."

Jones laughed at the odd carts, but when he saw how well they held together in the arid air, he traded his American horses and wagons for Indian horses and Red River carts and continued to Oregon.

The handcart pioneers bound for the Colorado goldfields were a redoubtable lot. Three or four men would load 100 pounds of gear into two-wheeled carts and push them over hill and dale to the Rocky Mountains.

The *Omaha Times* suggested to the handcart travelers, "If you're going to Pikes Peak, why don't you wait for grass?"

"What do we need grass for?" replied the handcarters, according to the newspaper. "We ain't got no stock."

"Yes, but since you're making asses of yourselves you might need it for food."

Even at that the handcarters couldn't compare to the team of young men who pulled a buggy westward during the Colorado Gold Rush. An eastern

dandy in a fine cloth coat, stovepipe hat, and patent leather shoes rode in the buggy behind the brawny youths.

A few years before, in his General Epistle of October, 1851, Brigham Young of the Church of Jesus Christ of Latter-day Saints pointed out that if the profane gold seekers could walk to California with their belongings in a wheelbarrow, then Mormons seeking a higher God than gold might do as well. He wrote:

"Yes, start from the Missouri River with Cows, handcarts, wheelbarrows, with little flour and no unnecessaries and come to this place quicker, and with less fatigue, than by following the heavy trains with their cumbrous herds which they are often obliged to drive miles to feed."

Under the direction of Chauncey Webb, a wagonwright, Mormon carpenters began the construction of the carts at Iowa City, Iowa, in the autumn of 1855. Young may have had some role in the design of the carts, which resembled the pushcarts used by peddlers in eastern cities. They were literally boxes on wheels set to the five-foot track of a wagon. The sidepieces extended into six-foot shafts joined in front by a crossbar, against which a man could push both his hands and his chest. The sides were either solid or made of slats.

Above: *Pushing and pulling handcarts, gold-hungry pioneers braved the West. "Hoofing it" was the only means of travel available to those pioneers who had no money for expensive wagons and livestock. Their plebeian wheels rolled west just as surely as did those of more fortunate pioneers.*

Left: *Gold fever struck people in the East with such fury that some loaded a few belongings into wheelbarrows and attempted to wheel their way across the plains and through the mountains. The extraordinary thing is that many of them made it, first to the California goldfields and later to those of Colorado.*

Family carts had hooped covers and were heavier and more solid than those intended solely for supplies. Some had iron axles or iron strips inserted into the hickory axle to make them wear longer. Some had thin iron tires, and others had tires of rawhide. Elm was used for hubs, white oak for spokes and rims, and ash for shafts and box. Well-seasoned wood from the bottoms along the Iowa River was used at first, but when this ran out green wood was substituted. It shrank and the carts fell apart, much to the discomfiture of the pioneers fated to pull the carts west.

When Mormon converts from England and Scandinavia arrived at Iowa City in the spring of 1856, the carts were not ready. Those converts who had any wagon-building skills pitched in and helped finish the carts, which were completed at the end of another four weeks. On June 9 and June 11 the first brigade of men, women, and children—497 people with 100 carts—set out on the 1,200-mile trudge. They sang a song:

> Who cares to go with the wagons?
> Not we who are free and strong;
> Our faith and arms, with a right good will,
> Shall pull our carts along.

The first of the handcart brigades reached Utah in about the same amount of time a wagon train would have taken. The second brigade arrived in good season in the fall, but the Martin and Willie companies, which both started in July, were caught in Wyoming by the first fall snows. From the start the ill-fated pioneers were short of supplies; they lived on a pound of flour a person each day. At Fort Laramie they traded their watches and rings for what provisions they could afford, but they still had to cut their rations to three-quarters pound of flour, then to one-half pound, and in time still lower.

The handcarts broke on the rocky trails. On October 19 the snow caught the pioneers at the Red Buttes. To cross the Platte they had to wade through icy water. A blizzard blew up. They pushed and pulled their carts through the swirling snow up the Sweetwater River towards the Devil's Gate. The higher the brigade climbed, the deeper the snow.

After each cruel night men, women, and children were found frozen in their thin blankets. Unable to go any farther, they dug away the snow with frying pans and tin plates so that they could put up their tents. The party was marooned. By November 18, when supply wagons sent from Salt Lake City by Young reached them, at least 200 Saints had died of starvation and exposure. Even so, from 1856 to 1861 some 4,000 Mormons journeyed to Salt Lake in ten handcart companies, with 662 carts.

The Mormons traveled with some of the lightest vehicles to roll into the West. James Frazier Reed of Sangamon County, Illinois, traveled with one of the heaviest. When Reed, a furniture manufacturer, decided to emigrate, he turned his factory

Mormon emigrants from England and Scandinavia pulled handcarts to the Promised Land beyond the mountains. In June, 1856, the first brigade of 497 men, women, and children set out with 100 carts on the 1,200-mile trek. They arrived in Utah in about the same time it would have taken a wagon train.

An emigrant wagon train on its way to Salt Lake City about 1866 paused in Utah's Echo Canyon. One of the Mormon handcart brigades once paused in the canyon so that a woman could give birth to a baby. The pioneers named the child "Echo."

over to making a double-deck wagon with steps leading down the side from the upper floor. There was a sheet-iron stove, with a stovepipe thrusting up through the canvas cover. There were built-in shelves, boxes, drawers, and a place for a rocking chair, in which Reed's mother-in-law, Grandma Sarah Keyes, was going to ride to her new home in California. Reed's daughter Virginia later named the wagon the "Pioneer Palace Car."

Reed and his family started out for California with the Donner Party in 1846 and suffered all of that company's tragic experiences. Sarah Keyes died in Kansas and was buried near Alcove Springs, but eight oxen dragged the huge vehicle far into the West. While the wagon was crossing the Wasatch Mountains of Utah, its canvas covering caught on the wall of a narrow gorge and was ripped. At Silver

Island, a great rock that rises like an island in the desert, the "Pioneer Palace Car" had to be abandoned. Slowly disintegrating, it lay in the shade cast by the rock until 1927, when its remains were discovered by Charles E. Davis, who was tracing the route of the Donner Party.

There were other wagons on the western trails with stovepipes peaking through their white tops as an indication that a cookstove was within. Peter Winne rode to Denver in 1863 over the central overland road in a wagon built so that it not only carried a sheet-iron stove, but projected six inches on each side of the box, enabling people to sleep crosswise in it at night. The wagon floor was carpeted.

Not all the wheels that rolled into the West carried emigrants and their gear. Some counted miles. Understandably pioneers were passionately

Romanticized pictures published in the East showed westering wagon trains passing through the Rocky Mountains. They made the journey seem like a carefree lark. In reality wagon trains avoided the mountains as much as possible, because they inflicted the cruelest of suffering on both man and beast.

WAGON TRAIN by N. C. Wyeth

WAGON BOSS by Charles M. Russell

PIKE'S PEAK OR BUST by Benton Clark
HARMSEN'S WESTERN AMERICANA

ORE WAGON by N. C. Wyeth

interested in the number of miles they covered each day. There were often furious arguments as to the exact distance they had gone, with the optimists claiming more miles and the pessimists fewer. Mormon William Clayton told about such an argument in his journal entry of May 8, 1847:

I have counted the revolutions of a wagon wheel to tell the exact distance we have traveled. The reason why I have taken this method which is somewhat tedious, is because there is generally a difference of two and sometimes four miles in a day's travel between my estimation and that of some others, and they have all thought I underrated it. This morning I determined to take pains to know for a certainty how far we travel today. Accordingly I measured the circumference of the nigh hind wheel of one of Brother Kimball's wagons being the one I sleep in, in charge of Philo Johnson. I found the wheel 14 feet 8 inches in circumference, not varying one eighth of an inch. I then calculated how many revolutions it would require for one mile and found it precisely 360 not varying one fraction which somewhat astonished me. I have counted the whole revolutions during the day's travel and I find it to be a little over eleven and a quarter miles,—twenty revolutions over.

Clayton was nursing a toothache as he walked behind the wagon counting the turns of the wheel. No wonder that he thought up a device to do the job. He proposed "fixing up a set of wooden cogwheels to the hub of a wagon wheel in such order as to tell the exact number of miles that we travel each day."

By May 16 Clayton and mechanic Appleton Harmon had perfected the gadget. He jotted in his journal, "About noon today Brother Appleton Harmon completed the machinery on the wagon called a 'roadometer' by adding a wheel to revolve once in ten miles, showing each mile and also each quarter mile we travel, and then casing the whole over so as to secure it from the weather."

A model of the "roadometer" is displayed in the museum at Scotts Bluff National Monument in Nebraska, not far from where the original device was first attached to a wagon.

No matter whether the miles were counted or not, they were full of trouble. Stumps left in the

A wagon train bound from Saint Joseph, Missouri, to Boise, Idaho, stretches out across the plains. It is 1862, when crossing the plains became more dangerous than ever. The Indians grew bolder with the whites fighting one another in the Civil War.

Above: *The Oregon Trail left the Red Buttes on the North Platte River in Wyoming for the Sweetwater River. Today this strategic point in the settling of the West is known as Bessemer Bend.*

Below: *East of Boulder, Colorado, covered wagons wait to ford the South Platte. Sometimes high waters held up the wagons, so that several hundred would gather. Afterwards pioneer families remembered these respites on the trail, when they could be sociable before starting on the next leg of their journey.*

Above: *Caught in the high mountain passes by an early snow, emigrants huddle in their wagons. This picture represents an eastern artist's conception of the tragic end that befell a family traveling with the Donner Party. A covered wagon provided very little shelter against the blasts of winter.*

Below: *By 1867 Salt Lake City was a flourishing town on the road to California. Wagon trains stopped to re-outfit, buy supplies, make repairs, or gather courage for the next hard stretch across the hot and dry Great Basin to the west.*

MARSHALL'S FERRY AND TRADING POST. PALMETTO. KANSAS TERRITORY. 1857

At first pioneers forded the Big Blue River at Independence Crossing (present-day Marysville) in Kansas. Oxen and wagons plunged down steep banks to cross what Sir Richard Burton, the English adventurer, called "a pretty little stream, brisk and clear as a crystal." Later a ferryboat took the wagons across the stream.

trail by wagon drivers who had cut a tree off just low enough to let their own vehicles clear would grab a low axle.

"Well, I'll be stumped!" entered a driver's language to describe a situation from which there seemed to be no way out. Frequently an axle snapped at a blow from a stump. Then there had better be a spare hanging beneath the wagon; otherwise the wagon had to be abandoned, or cut down to the dimensions of a cart. At least one pair of men going to the mines of California found another reason to make carts from their wagon. Determined to part because of a quarrel, they sawed the wagon in half, and each attached a pair of oxen to the cart he had received as his half of the partnership and drove off to the West.

On sharp turns tongues also snapped. Axletrees broke in chuckholes. Sometimes the entire wagon stuck in hub-deep mud. Thomas Scott came upon a man whose wagon was sunk in the prairie mud.

"Well, you are in a bad fix," he sympathized.

"Oh, no," replied the driver without a trace of a smile. "I am all right, but there are two wagons below mine, and those fellows down there are having a hell of a time."

The brakes on covered wagons were not very good, and the only way to lower a wagon down a steep hill was to make a windlass. At Windlass Hill, looking down into Ash Hollow, Nebraska, pioneers staked a wagon to the ground at the top of the hill and jacked up the hind wheels so they would turn without moving the wagon. A rope was wound around the hub of one wheel, and its other end was fastened to the wagon being lowered. A team of oxen was positioned at the front of the latter wagon to keep its tongue from dragging and to guide it as it descended. Men seized hold of the spokes of the upended wheel.

"Ready! Go!"

The heavily loaded wagon inched down the hill —unless the rope broke. Then it careened to the bottom and was usually smashed beyond use. In 1853 an emigrant train crossing the Naches Pass through the Cascade Mountains of Washington discovered that the descent from the summit was more than 1,000 feet at an angle of sixty degrees. The wagons were eased down the steep slope by ropes, but the ropes were not long enough to reach the bottom.

"Kill one of the poorest of my steers, and make a rope of its hide," said James Biles, "and if that is

Above: *Lane's Fort looks down from atop a Kansas hill on an emigrant wagon. The driver trudges beside his team. Most men employed what Abraham Lincoln called "Shank's Mare" to walk into the West. Only the sick and the weak rode in the wagons.*

Below: *Frontier painter-photographer William H. Jackson came upon these wagons crossing the South Platte River near Julesburg, Colorado, on the Oregon Trail. As the heavily loaded wagons roll down to the river crossing, an Indian party behind the teepees approaches with a load mounted on a travois.*

not enough, kill another." Three of Biles' oxen had to be slaughtered before the hide rope could be made long enough to lower the wagons safely to the bottom of the descent.

The Barlow Road down Laurel Hill in Oregon was cut five to seven feet into the earth by rough-locked wagons. Veteran wagoners chopped down a small tree about ten inches in diameter and forty feet long and chained it to the rear axle in order to slow the wagon's plunge down the slope. At the foot of the hill a wagoner had to drag a tree out of the road, where it had been left by the wagoner before him. He in turn left his tree for the next man to pull out of the way.

Even a wrecked wagon still had value. On the high plains, where wood was scarce, it furnished fuel for a cooking or warming fire. At times there was plenty of such costly firewood. One traveler counted at least 1,000 abandoned wagons in a forty-two-mile stretch of trail. Spokes could be used to make pack-saddles. A wagon box might provide material for a grave marker or for a coffin. When two young women died of typhoid fever while members of a wagon train following the Humboldt River in Nevada, they were buried on the trail. The wagons were driven over their graves to hide them from the Indians, who otherwise might have dug up the bodies in search of useful clothing.

On a happier note, Enoch W. Conyers, a pioneer of 1852, celebrated the Fourth of July with his party in the Sweetwater Valley of Wyoming. They took apart the wagon beds to form long tables for the feast prepared by the women. The tables were decorated with evergreens and wild flowers, and Virgil Ralston, from Quincy, Illinois, climbed atop one table to give the Independence Day oration. The hubs of a broken wagon helped another party celebrate Independence Day at Independence Rock. They filled the hubs of broken wagon wheels with gunpowder and put them inside cracks in the rock. The pioneers deemed that the explosions they touched off were a fitting salute to the United States.

Wagon tongues were equally useful. In camp a young couple could spend the evening sitting on a wagon tongue, holding hands. Young Henry Stine wrote a letter home to his mother from Fort Laramie in 1850, "sitting on a wagon tongue, my Port Folio on my lap." Conyers described a somewhat different use for wagon tongues. There had been a murder in the company ahead of his on the Oregon Trail. Conyers reported that, finding the murderer guilty, "the company ran two wagons together, elevating the tongues in the shape of the letter 'A,' tying them together. On this improvised gallows the defendant was hung until life was pronounced extinct."

The weight of a wagon and its cargo was a crucial matter as the train pressed farther and farther west and the draft animals became worn out. Randolph Marcy urged:

"Wagons with six mules should never, on a long journey over the prairies, be loaded with over 2000 pounds, unless grain is transported, when an additional thousand pounds may be taken, provided it is fed out daily to the team. When grass constitutes the only forage, 2000 pounds is deemed a sufficient load."

Most family wagons were overloaded with furniture, iron stoves, and all sorts of other household

Left, top: *Register Cliff, southeast of Guernsey, Wyoming, is at the end of ranch roads today, but once it was a natural landmark on the Oregon Trail. Pioneers registered their names on the limestone cliff as early as 1842. Over 500 pioneer names can still be read. Higher on the cliff is a colony of mudbirds' nests.*

Left, bottom: *Independence Rock on the Sweetwater River in Wyoming was named by fur trappers who celebrated the Fourth of July there in 1825. Wagon trains that arrived at the rock during the first few days of July often stayed on to celebrate the nation's birthday. The pioneers filled the hubs of broken wagon wheels with gunpowder and placed them in cracks in the rock. The loud bangs seemed appropriate as salutes to the nation. Most of the emigrants traveling along the Oregon Trail scratched their names on the rock, and there are still some 50,000 inscriptions to be read. Among the names is that of Jim Bridger, but someone else must have cut it for him, since he could not write.*

Above: *The West seems bright with promise in this illustration from 1869. As covered wagons press onwards along the trail, a pioneer family stops by the wayside to feed the horses and to cook a meal over a fire built of wood. Even good drinking water flows by the site, ready for a woman to dip it up.*

Right, top: *Wagon wheels following the Oregon Trail left such deep ruts in the sandstone near Wyoming's Register Cliff that their tracks will be seen for generations to come.*

Right, bottom: *West of Split Rock, Wyoming, the Oregon Trail cuts through the dry high country. This often scorching stretch of the journey west was made easier for pioneers because at Split Rock there was an ice slough beneath a layer of peat, at the depth of a man's arm. Henry Tappan, a forty-niner, wrote that he found the ice ideal for a julep to take the heat out of a broiling hot day.*

goods that a woman was loath to leave behind. If she could actually get the things to her new home, they would be invaluable. The trails were strewn with precious articles that had been discarded, usually after their weight had exhausted the draft animals. Some pioneers buried their belongings close to the trail in the hope that they could come back and get the articles later. A few threw them out of the wagons in a rage, but most stacked them in neat piles to which they affixed a sign inviting more fortunate people with space in their wagons to help themselves.

Even so, all manner of odd cargoes found their way across the plains and through the mountains by emigrant wagon. In 1847 Henderson Luelling managed to bring a wagonload of infant fruit trees, set in small boxes of earth, all the way from Salem, Iowa, to the Willamette Valley of Oregon, where he planted them and thus started the fruit industry in the Pacific Northwest. The Alsatian settlers who founded Castroville, Texas, brought along a complete building stocked with provisions on a big cart. A Missouri man loaded a hive of bees onto his wagon and moved west with it over the Oregon Trail. A

Above: *Two wagon trains camp near one another, forming a large corral. Some fortunate families have erected tents. Others will sleep in or under the wagons. The stock are moving out to pasture and all is tranquil. Later in life many of the emigrants looked back on their often arduous trip west and remembered the deep feeling of happiness that came at the end of a hard day, when families and their friends gathered around their campfires and talked, played practical jokes, and listened to the scraping of a fiddle or the strumming of a banjo.*

Right: *At the end of a day's journey the wagons were arranged in a circle to thwart possible Indian attacks and to keep the draft stock from wandering off. A touching vignette of untroubled family life is presented in the lower left corner, while the opposite side of the illustration shows some of the horses galloping into the corral from the prairies where they were grazing.*

westering publisher and his staff burdened two wagons with printing presses and rolled out across the plains to Denver, where they founded the *Rocky Mountain News*. In 1843 William Baldridge tried to take a mill to California. He took it apart, packed it in boxes, and placed it on a wagon. Mountain man Joseph Walker, who was serving as the party's guide, tried to get the mill west from Fort Hall with the first emigrant wagons to enter California. Faced with exhausted mules, dwindling food, and the possibility of an Indian attack, Baldridge buried the mill in the sands of the Owens Valley desert, where a prospector accidentally discovered it some twenty-five years later. Another wagon train was at the same time a funeral cortege: William Keil carried along the body of his son Willie all the way from Missouri to Washington Territory.

Every night the pioneers arranged their wagons in corrals to defend themselves against Indian attack and to confine the livestock, just as the freighting caravans on the Santa Fe Trail had done. In 1876 Jesse Applegate, a pioneer on the Oregon Trail, told the Oregon Pioneer Association what an emigrants' corral was like:

"The corral is a circle one hundred yards deep, formed with wagons connected strongly with each other; the wagon in the rear being connected with the wagon in front by its tongue and ox chains. It is a strong barrier that the most vicious ox cannot break, and in case of an attack of the Sioux would be no contemptible intrenchment."

Sometimes the corral was circular or oblong in shape. An opening was left for the livestock to be driven in or out, but at night it could be closed with a wagon tongue. Sometimes the corral was U-shaped.

The dispute as to whether oxen or mules were best to pull a wagon never was fully settled among the freighters of the Southwest. And it still raged among the emigrants. Horses, most emigrants agreed,

were too expensive in the first place, and they had to have grain to be at their best. They were most useful in scouting. Marcy wrote:

There has been much discussion regarding the relative merits of mules and oxen for prairie traveling, and the question is yet far from being settled. Upon good firm roads, in a populated country, where grain can be procured, I should unquestionably give the preference to mules, as they travel faster, and endure the heat of summer much better than oxen; and if the journey be not over 1000 miles, and the grass abundant, even without grain, I think mules would be preferable. But when the march is to extend 1500 or 2000 miles, or over a rough sandy or muddy road, I believe young oxen will endure better than mules; they will, if properly managed, keep in better condition, and perform the journey in an equally brief space of time. Besides, they are much more economical, a team of six mules costing six hundred dollars, while an eight-ox team only costs upon the frontier about two hundred dollars. Oxen are much less liable to be stampeded and driven off by Indians, and can be pursued and overtaken by horsemen; and, finally, they can, if necessary, be used for beef.

Emigrants from the South seemed to favor the mule, but those from the North favored the ox. Cows were rarely used except by the Mormons, who—in order to provide milk on the trail—made a general rule calling for a yoke of oxen and a yoke of milk cows to haul each wagon. One family lost an ox, either to an Indian raiding party or to exhaustion. They hitched the remaining ox to a mule, and the two animals took an unprecedented liking for one another. They pulled their wagon in true comradery.

No matter which draft animal the emigrants favored, however, they could be certain that hardships along the trail would wear their animals so thin that, as the saying went, it would take two of them to make a shadow.

When an emigrant wagon had reached its last camp, it still had its uses. It could live out an honorable life as a farm or freight wagon. The citizens of Casper, Wyoming, built their first houses out of their wagon boxes and canvas. George W. Stokes, one of

Above: *An evening with a Gold Rush wagon train was a time for rest and for the fiddle. Often there was a sadness born of the weary miles that separated the men from their families in the East.*

Left: *Emigrants in this colorful early painting have blundered into an Indian attack. The battle rages, but there is little of the real terror and death that Indians sometimes inflicted upon a hapless wagon train.*

four men who reached South Dakota in December, 1875, remembered, "We cut up parts of the wagon bodies to make doors, and two boot legs provided the material for the hinges." They used the wagon sheets on their beds. The first merchant who arrived in Belton, Texas, in 1850 converted his wagon into a store right next door to the first saloon, which was a barrel of bourbon and a tin cup under a shade tree. There is a venerable old plow in the Arizona Museum in Phoenix that was fashioned from the iron tire of a pioneer wagon wheel.

A nation moved westward on the wheels of the covered wagon, but now very few of them are left.

For years an original emigrant wagon stood close to the ruts of the Oregon Trail at Scotts Bluff National Monument, but a reproduction made at the shops of Silver Dollar City, Missouri, has taken its place. Once a day during the summer Mort Davis, who teaches history at Nebraska Western College, demonstrates how to change and grease a wagon wheel. The jack he uses has endured for more than a century, made in 1876 either by Murphy or by Studebaker, but he makes sure that a modern hydraulic jack is holding up the load before he risks removing the wheel. The past has a way of falling on a man.

Left: *Emmanuel H. Custer of New Rumley, Ohio, father of Lt. Col. George Armstrong Custer of Little Big Horn fame, was a celebrated wagonmaker. He built this wagon in 1821, and it was used many times by the Custer family on western trails. Today it is kept at Lincoln's New Salem State Park near Spring-field, Illinois. From time to time schoolchildren are loaded in its historic bed and the old wagon is drawn creaking around the park by a pair of oxen hitched to the tongue.*

Below: *Sodbusters settling in the Loup Valley of Nebraska in 1886 still rode from railhead to their homesteads in covered wagons. The wagons were more comfortable than those of earlier settlers and more often than not they were pulled by horses, which were much too expensive for most of the early pioneers.*

"Pennsylvanians Going East; And don't you forget it" is the motto of this *"busted"* group of pioneers, who have decided that their native Keystone State has more to offer than the West. There was an ebb flow of one-time emigrants back to the states from which they came.

WHEELS FOR THE FRONTIER ARMY

LIEUTENANT FRANK BALDWIN loaded his troops into Army escort wagons from which he had removed the cloth covers. With the mules at a gallop, the wagons bore down on a Kiowa village. The soldiers fired over the mules' heads. The tactic caught the Indians by surprise, and Baldwin's attack was a success.

The four-horse or four-mule escort wagon and its military predecessor on the western frontier, the six-mule wagon, were among the hardiest vehicles ever to roll west of the Mississippi. Both of them were logical descendants of the celebrated Conestoga wagon, although much smaller and lighter because of their off-the-road use in rough country.

The Conestoga itself saw military service on the westering frontier beginning in 1755, when Benjamin Franklin made possible the hiring of wagons and teams from Pennsylvania farmers to transport supplies for Major General Braddock's disastrous expedition. The Conestoga saw service in the American Revolution, the War of 1812, and the Mexican War. When General Kearny's army moved out of Fort Leavenworth, Kansas, on June 26, 1846, bound for Santa Fe, over 100 wagons carrying supplies went first, guarded by two companies of dragoons.

Not all the wagons used by the Army in the West up to the time of the Mormon War of 1857–1858 were actually Conestogas. Many were imitations made in Philadelphia or in Pittsburgh. In his *Five Years a Dragoon* Percival G. Lowe complains of the quality of the Pittsburgh wagons that

served in the Utah campaign. The timber was not properly seasoned, and the wagon boxes and wheels pulled apart in the dry air as the wagons floundered through the rocks and sand. The soldiers treasured stray pieces of pine, and every evening, after reaching camp, they wedged them into warped boxes and tires. Often they worked until midnight. Even so, wagons fell apart on the trail and had to be abandoned.

From colonial days, when Franklin helped to acquire civilian Conestoga wagons for Braddock's campaign, civilian freighters carried most of the supplies to western Army posts in large freight wagons. Pre-eminent among the civilian freighters of the trans-Missouri West was the firm of Russell, Majors & Waddell. At the height of its business freighting to the Army, as well as to frontier mining camps and towns, the firm operated 6,200 wagons. Mostly made by Murphy, they were capable of carrying from 5,000 to 7,000 pounds of cargo apiece. If all the company's wagons were to form a single train over the plains, the column would be forty miles long. When Horace Greeley visited the Russell, Majors & Waddell headquarters at Leavenworth, Kansas, in 1859, he exclaimed, "Such acres of wagons! Such pyramids of extra axletrees! such herds of oxen! such regiments of drivers and other employees!"

Greeley was given to exclamations, but the facts justified his enthusiasm. At one time the company worked 75,000 head of oxen. The firm put some of

its cattle in winter pasture between the present-day Greeley, Colorado, and Buffalo, Wyoming.

"For two winters, those of 1857 and 1858, I wintered fifteen thousand head of heavy-work-oxen on the plains," William Russell wrote.

Civilian freighters may have carried the supplies to the frontier posts, but transportation on a campaign was the Army's problem, and the passing years saw a variety of vehicles manufactured for the Army. The six-mule Army wagon was introduced during the Civil War. Its sides were straight, but its side paneling turned up at the ends, giving it something of a Conestoga's nautical lines. A white wagon cover completed the wagon's resemblance to a miniature Conestoga. The toolbox was mounted on the front gate, and the feed trough was slung in the rear of the wagon.

Quartermaster Department specifications covered every detail. They required: "The body to be straight, three feet six inches wide, two feet deep, ten feet along the bottom, ten feet six inches at the top, sloping equally at each end."

Two "good coats of white lead, colored to a blue tint" must be applied to the outside of the body and to the feed trough. The inside of the body was to be given two coats of Venetian red paint, and the running gear was to have "two good coats of Venetian red, darkened to a chocolate color." The hubs and felloes were to be well pitched instead of painted, if the service intended for the vehicle made it desirable.

Each side of the wagon box was to be numbered and marked with "U.S.," and was to carry the name of the wagonmaker and the place of manufacture. Even the construction of the feed trough was provided for by exact specifications. A trough was to have "sides of yellow pine, to be four feet six inches long from out and out; the bottom and ends of oak, well ironed with a band of hoop iron around the top, one around each end and three between the ends."

It was stipulated that an extra kingbolt and two extra singletrees must accompany each wagon.

At first the driver rode atop the left near wheel mule on a Conestoga freighter's saddle, but later the

Left: *Army supply vehicles roll into the Alamo in San Antonio. Founded as a Franciscan mission in 1718, the Alamo served as a fort after 1793. Because of its role in Texas' struggle for independence from Mexico it became known as the "Cradle of Texas Liberty," and in 1849 it became the first U.S. fort in Texas.*

Below: *Louis Guenot from Quebec built a wooden bridge across the Platte in Wyoming in 1858. He charged fifty cents a crossing most of the time, but he would raise the fee to as much as five dollars if he thought he could get it. The Indians weren't concerned with the fees he charged, but they did not take kindly to the bridge. In 1861 Col. W. H. Collins brought the 115th Ohio to erect a post at the crossing, and there appeared to be little that the Indians could do about the situation. Then on July 26, 1865, Sgt. Amos J. Custard and twenty-three men set out with a westbound wagon train. The Indians attacked them within sight of the fort and all but three of the soldiers were killed. Lieutenant Caspar W. Collins, son of the colonel, dashed to the rescue with reinforcements, but just beyond the bridge a multitude of Indians ambushed them. The young officer was killed when he stopped to succor a fallen soldier, and the post was named Fort Caspar for the dead lieutenant. In 1867 Fort Caspar was abandoned, and the Indians burned both fort and bridge. The present-day city of Casper keeps alive the trooper's name, even if it is misspelled.*

Above: *Civilian freighters brought most of the supplies to the Army forts in the Old West, but when the soldiers campaigned in the field it was Army wagons that rolled with them. This scouting party of Company K, Nineteenth U.S. Infantry, is ready for action.*

Right, top: *Cannons of various types rolled into the West on wheels and played their part in the settling of the frontier. This cannon stands on the grounds of Fort Defiance, an outpost in Arizona.*

Right, bottom: *Soldiers at Fort Abraham Lincoln gather about a Gatling gun mounted on big wheels for mobility. Custer's Seventh Cavalry was based at this fort in Dakota Territory.*

Army mounted him on a western-style Morgan saddle with a horn on the pommel. There was no brake at first, and on steep grades the vehicle's descent could be slowed only by putting a rough lock on one of the wheels. In 1863 a single iron lever fastened to the brake beam by a chain or rope was installed on the wagons. Later a ratchet type was introduced. A large lever was placed near the left front of the box, where the driver mounted in the saddle could reach it. The lever was linked to the rear brake by an iron rod.

The six-mule wagon was present on almost every expedition against the Indians all the way along the embattled frontier. Buffalo Bill Cody noted that the Fifth Cavalry usually traveled with a full wagon train of seventy-five six-mule wagons, "ambulances," and pack mules. The largest six-mule wagon train ever assembled was doubtless the train that hauled the supplies for Lieutenant Colonel Custer's winter campaign against the Indians in 1868. There were 800 wagons, and the column was four miles long.

Above: *When the Custer Expedition to the Black Hills reached the Valley of Heart, in what is now North Dakota, their horses were allowed to graze under the watchful eyes of the troopers. Custer set out from Fort Abraham Lincoln during the summer of 1874 with 1,200 troops and a handful of scientists to see if there was gold in the Black Hills, which by treaty with the Sioux were off limits to whites. The expedition's supplies were transported by a fleet of military wagons, which may be seen in the background of this rare photograph taken by William H. Illingworth.*

Left: *Traveling in four columns for the best defense against possible Indian attack, the Custer Expedition to the Black Hills passes along what came to be the North Dakota-South Dakota state line. Photographer Illingworth accompanied the expedition and made this historic photograph, using a bulky camera and a glass plate. He first had to prepare a light-sensitive solution on the plate in a portable darkroom; then, after he had exposed the plate for ten to fifteen seconds, he developed the negative at once before the emulsion dried. Later he made prints from the negatives in his Saint Paul, Minnesota, studio. Years afterwards the original glass negatives were found in a Saint Paul attic. They are now in the South Dakota Historical Society Museum at Pierre.*

When Brig. Gen. Henry Carrington was sent to build forts to protect the Bozeman Trail against Red Cloud's Sioux, 220 vehicles, including both Dougherty ambulances and six-mule wagons, rolled north with him from Fort Laramie into the Powder River country. They carried supplies, tools, and gear, as well as the wives and children of the soldiers.

Captain James W. Powell and his twenty-six men had fourteen six-mule wagons with them when they set out on a wood-chopping expedition in the Big Horn Mountains, five miles away from Fort Kearny. Having felled a number of trees, the men removed the wagon boxes from the running gears, because only the gears were needed to haul the logs back to the post. As a precaution against Indian attack, Captain Powell directed the men to place the boxes end to end to form an egg-shaped corral. They stuffed the openings between the boxes with kegs, logs, and ox yokes.

On the morning of August 2, 1867, Red Cloud's warriors attacked the corral. The soldiers hastily piled sacks of grain atop the wagon boxes to help stop arrows and bullets, and closed the openings left in the rampart with wagons on wheels. Thirty-two soldiers fought off the attacking Sioux. The wagon boxes deflected the arrows, if not the bullets. Thanks to the deadly efficiency of the new breech-loading rifles that they had recently been issued and to the sturdiness of the wagon boxes, the small band of soldiers held out for three full hours, until Maj. Benjamin F. Smith arrived with reinforcements. The Wagon Box Fight became one of the most talked-about episodes in the Sioux War.

The canvas-topped escort wagon, drawn by either four horses or four mules, appeared in the West in the 1870s. It preserved the color scheme of the six-mule wagon until the last years of the nineteenth century, when the Army's pervasive olive

Fort Bayard, New Mexico, provided sheds for its vehicles and stables for its horses. A gate led to the untrammeled open country that the fort was designed to protect.

drab took over. The escort wagon was six inches shorter than the six-mule wagon and two or three inches narrower. Its sides were straight.

The driver sat on the inside seat and drove the teams by the four-horse-rein method. He was treated to unheard-of luxury—elliptical springs beneath his seat, and a footboard. Three extra seats, also with springs, could be installed inside the wagon to make it into a troop carrier.

The escort wagon featured patent flange iron wheel hubs, spokes set closer together, iron axles, and iron wheel nuts, which replaced the traditional linchpins. It proved to be such a fine wagon that the Army not only kept it in service throughout the last decades of fighting on the Indian frontier, but took it to France during World War I, where it hauled either a dozen soldiers or cargoes of supplies from railhead to the front lines.

Both the six-mule wagon and the escort wagon were made by various manufacturers to Army orders, but the Studebaker Company of South Bend, Indiana, made the lion's share of them after 1858, when the Studebaker brothers won their first big Army order for 100 wagons to transport supplies on the plains. They promised to build the wagons of seasoned wood in six months' time, and they were able to complete the task in three months by drying the wood in a specially constructed kiln.

Easily the best collection of vehicles used on the Great Plains by the U.S. Army is at Fort Sill, Oklahoma. On a single visit it is possible to see not only an escort wagon, but also a U.S. Army buckboard, a wagonette, a canopy-top phaeton such as the commanding officer of the post would have used, an ice wagon from 1850, an ambulance, a mountain wagon, a three-seater roof break, and a very well preserved Conestoga—a fascinating pageant of military transportation.

Right: *A stage's military escort poses on the western frontier. A stage or a Dougherty wagon, the latter called an "ambulance" by the Army, might carry a very important personage from Washington, D.C., a visiting general, or the payroll for the fort.*

Below: *The officers of the Seventh Cavalry and their wives strike appropriate attitudes for the photographer who visited Fort Abraham Lincoln in Dakota Territory. Third from the left, striking the most gallant attitude of all, is Lt. Col. George Armstrong Custer, and just beyond the next officer is Elizabeth, his wife. Custer had an "ambulance" fixed up for Elizabeth so that the leather backs of the seats could be unstrapped at the sides and lowered to form a bed. There was even a pocket for her needlework, a book, and a lunch box.*

The ambulance displayed at Fort Sill was made by the Studebaker Company to transport the wounded, but not all vehicles called ambulances in the West were intended for the injured or the sick. To a soldier on the plains an "ambulance" might be a buckboard, a mountain wagon, or some other vehicle used to transport passengers, but most likely it would be a Dougherty spring wagon.

The Dougherty wagon, sometimes called the Army limousine or the "avalanche," was drawn by four mules. It was open in the front so that the driver could sit beneath a canvas awning and keep a practiced eye on the road and on his often recalcitrant team. Wives and children of the officers often rode in them. Martha Summerhayes described a Dougherty wagon in her account of life in frontier Arizona with her soldier husband:

"A Dougherty wagon or in common army parlance an ambulance was secured for me to travel in. This vehicle had a large body, with two seats facing each other and a seat outside for the driver. The inside of the wagon could be closed if desired, by canvas sides and back which rolled up and down and by a curtain which dropped behind the driver's seat. So I was enabled to have some degree of privacy."

A person climbed into the wagon through a side door. There was a covered baggage rack in the rear. The vehicle was considered the last word in convenience. Lieutenant Colonel Custer's wife Elizabeth had an "ambulance" fixed up so the leather backs of the seats could be unstrapped at the sides and laid down to make a bed. There was a pocket for her needlework, a book, and a box for her lunch.

"It was quite a complete house of itself," she was pleased to report.

Mrs. Custer might have demanded that her husband's troopers give her wagon the standard winterizing that was provided for Army wagons on the plains. To shelter men and cargo against blizzards, the wagon ends were built up with boards. A hinged door was set in the back. The wagon covers were doubled, and a small sheet-iron stove was put inside with a pipe peaking through the tarp.

The Army paymaster accompanied the payroll in a stagecoach guarded by troopers. The soldiers at Fort Meade, Dakota Territory, eagerly awaited this shipment, which was setting out from Deadwood. Dougherty wagons were also used to carry the Army pay.

At a western fort such as Fort Leavenworth, dependents also rode in the "break," so called because the high seats break from the top of the wagon bed. The break was also originally used to break teams. Since the driver sat high above the flying hoofs of the horses being trained to harness, he was considered to be safe. The same high seats gave a soldier's family a good view of cavalry on parade or any other event at the fort.

The wagonette was still another type of Army vehicle used by dependents. Similar to horse-drawn city buses in the East, the wagonette possessed glass windows. Its entrance was at the rear, and its seats lined the sides. Army families rode in wagonettes from the post to the nearest town on shopping trips or other excursions.

The Army paymaster traveled in a Dougherty wagon with his currency-stuffed leather wallet under the seat. Visiting congressmen, generals, and other dignitaries from the East were carried about in the Dougherty wagon, and out of Cheyenne in the late 1860s and early 1870s it was used by the government to carry mail and express, as well as civilian passengers under the management of the military.

Vehicles for transporting the sick and wounded were a different matter. At the time of the Mexican War the Army favored a one-horse ambulance cart. This blockish vehicle, covered with a canvas tarp, had elliptical springs intended to absorb the jounces and jolts of the trail, but the springs only emphasized each lurch of the cart. A wounded man preferred to be transported in almost any other vehicle. For the most part the injured were loaded onto springless wagons. A layer of hay or straw, or, if neither was available, brush, was put down on the floor and covered with a blanket. The wounded found some rough comfort atop the blanket.

On the western frontier the Army employed both the single-seater and the two-seater buckboard. There is a good example of the two-seater at Fort Sill. Gillett Griswold, director of the Fort Sill museum, notes that the U.S. Army buckboard was an American invention, developed for rough use.

"Its distinctive feature is that it lacks a body and springs," he comments. "Instead, long elastic boards are fastened securely to the front and rear axles and the seats are mounted thereon. The hickory slats of buckboards sprang and bucked from one end of the continent to the other as the settlements spread."

The U.S. Army mountain wagon was another rugged vehicle. It was equipped with springs and oversized brakes to handle the steep grades encountered in the mountain country. There was a luggage rack at the rear, and a canvas top could be attached in bad weather.

A commanding officer might use the mountain wagon in the field, but during garrison duty at a western fort such as Fort Leavenworth, he most likely rode about in a phaeton, a military adaptation of the four-wheeled vehicle with open sides that was named for Phaëthon, who in the Greek myth insisted on driving his father Helios' sun-chariot. The C.O. could make sharper turns in his phaeton than people in other vehicles could manage, because the body frame of his vehicle was higher under the seat than in other places. This gave the front wheels an unusual clearance.

A vehicle needed all the maneuverability it possessed when it fell into the hands of young Capt. Ulysses S. Grant, who in 1853 was the commanding officer of Company F, Fourth U.S. Infantry, at Fort Humboldt in northern California. Bored with garrison duty, Grant drove his buggy to the general store at nearby Eureka, where he basked in the company of James Talbot Ryan, storekeeper and Irish story-teller extraordinary. Having liberally sampled of the whiskey barrel that Ryan kept behind the counter, Grant hitched three buggies in tandem and drove them back to the fort at breakneck speed.

Military wagons sometimes carried soldiers as an escort for a stagecoach on an Indian-infested part of the Santa Fe Trail. Either infantrymen or dismounted horsemen rode in the wagons, which were supposed to furnish them with something of a bulwark in case of attack. This didn't keep the Kiowa from attacking both the mail wagon and its escort wagons at Cold Springs, Oklahoma, in 1859. The troops, wagon bulwark or no, were pinned down for several hours by the sharpshooting Indians.

A military wagon also saw service which was far less heroic. Soldiers could remove the covers and bows so that the wagon beds could be used for hauling stone, sand, lime, wood, brick, and other bulk cargoes. At Fort Leavenworth on October 4, 1841, Col. Richard B. Mason, the C.O., ordered Lt. Thomas Swords, Jr., the quartermaster, to put the wagons to work removing manure from the stables. At the same time a boat from Saint Louis arrived at the landing with a supply of flour. The boat's crew unloaded the flour onto the wharf. Because he feared that the rains might fall and ruin the flour before it could be moved, Swords attempted to divert his wagons to moving flour instead of manure. When the C.O. insisted that he stick to the manure, he wrote a bitter letter to Major General Jesup, quartermaster general in Washington. The manure had accumulated for months, said the lieutenant, and could wait to be moved. A rain would ruin the flour left out in the open on the wharf, but it was not likely to ruin the manure.

Military wagons on the frontier often had to travel over rudimentary roads, as the following story shows. At Fort Hoskins in 1856, young Phil Sheridan cleared a road across the mountains from Kings Valley to the Siletz River. In his *Personal Memoirs* Sheridan describes the obstacles his soldiers encountered in making the road:

The point at which the road was to cross the range was rough and precipitous, but the principal difficulty in making it would be from heavy timber on the mountains that had been burned over years and years before, until nothing was left but limbless trunks of dead trees—firs and pines—that had fallen from time to time until the ground was matted with huge logs from five to eight feet in diameter. These could not be chopped with axes nor sawed by any ordinary means, therefore we had to burn them into suitable lengths, and drag the sections to either side of the roadway with from four to six yoke of oxen.

Finally, when the road was presumed to be finished, Sheridan sent a wagon over it loaded with 1,500 pounds of freight. Six yoke of oxen pulled the vehicle, but about seven miles from the beginning of the road it stuck at the foot of a steep hill. Sheridan hurried to the scene. His *Memoirs* explain how he got the oxen moving:

Taking up a whip myself, I directed the men to lay on their gads, for each man had supplied himself with a flexible hickory withe in the early stages of the trip, to start the team, but this course did not move the wagon nor have much effect on the demoralized oxen; but following as a last resort an example I heard of on a former occasion, that brought into use the rough language of the country, I induced the oxen to move with alacrity, and the wagon and contents were speedily carried to the summit. The whole trouble was at once revealed: the oxen had been broken and trained by a man who, when they were in a pinch, had encouraged them by his frontier vocabulary, and they could not realize what was expected of them under extraordinary conditions until they heard familiar and possibly profanely urgent phrases. I took the wagon to its destination, but as it was not brought back, even in all the time I was stationed in that country, I think comment on the success of my road is unnecessary.

It seems reasonable that if a rugged military wagon could not get through, the road was no road at all.

The Twenty-fifth Regiment of the Army Infantry followed crude western roads and trails on bicycles. The men claimed that they could get into action while other troopers were still rounding up their horses.

FREIGHTING TO THE MINES

MORE THAN 600 freight wagons lumbered over the Mullan Road during the time when it was the hell-for-leather route from Fort Benton at the headwaters of navigation on the Missouri River to the Montana gold camps. When our family hiked over part of the Mullan Road through the hills in back of Fort Benton, one of the boys found a hinge from an old wagon lying beside the still remaining ruts.

Beyond Fort Shaw the Mullan Road is now a ranch road. We drove along the road between two buttes to abandoned St. Peter's Mission, where a double row of trees leads to tumbled walls. Near the old walls we discovered three vintage freight wagons and extra wheels rotting in the sun. Not many of the old freight wagons are left, and these old wagons will not last much longer.

Once there were thousands of freight wagons transporting supplies to frontier mining camps and towns and hauling out the ore. On the roads of the Comstock Lode, the wagons were often so thick that if a driver pulled out of line, he might have to wait a good part of a day to get back in. In Deadwood, South Dakota, at the height of the mining boom, Main Street was so congested with ore and freight wagons that traffic ground to a stop. Daring pedestrians crossed the street by climbing through and over the wagons.

The wagons that operated on the mining frontier were made by such manufacturers as Murphy, Espenscheidt, and later Kern in Saint Louis, Missouri; Cooper in Dubuque, Iowa; Schuttler in Jack-

son, Michigan; and Studebaker, whose wagon plant in South Bend, Indiana, eventually surpassed all the others in production. There were a few western manufacturers, such as Bain at Cheyenne, that made wagons for one mining field or another, and there were strange vehicles such as new versions of the windwagon—first introduced on the plains by Windwagon Thomas for the Santa Fe trade—and the steamwagon. There were the four-horse ore wagons used in Colorado camps and fourteen-horse wagons to haul heavy mine machinery. The wagons that carried supplies and sometimes complete stamping mills to the gold and silver mines of Nevada and Idaho were so huge that they were drawn by eighteen to twenty horses or mules, guided by a jerk line. Some California ore wagons had boxes two times as high as a man and wheels one and a half times the size of a man.

As the wagons reached the ultimate in practical size, trailers were added. In Arizona twenty-four mules or horses were required to pull a wagon and its trailer. Three wagons joined together by very short tongues became common in the California goldfields.

The largest vehicles of all were the famous borax wagons that hauled some 2.5 million pounds of borax yearly between 1883 and 1888 over the 165 miles separating Death Valley, California, and the railhead at Mojave. They accomplished this without a single breakdown. The wagons were called twenty-mule-team wagons, but in actuality they

Above: *In 1876 Deadwood, South Dakota, was a rip-roaring mining town where wagons and coaches could cause a traffic jam. At the height of the mining boom Deadwood's Main Street was often so congested with ore and freight wagons that traffic ground to a halt. A daredevil pedestrian could cross the street by climbing through and over the wagons.*

Right: *Death Valley Scotty and his wife presided over some of the hottest and driest land in the world. Death Valley Scotty's yarns about the twenty-mule-team borax wagons never let on that in reality the twenty-mule teams contained eighteen mules and two horses. The horses were given the wheel positions because they were both stronger and more obedient than the mules. The famous borax wagons, hooked in tandem, hauled some 2.5 million pounds of borax every year between 1883 and 1888 over the 165 miles from Death Valley, California, to the railhead at Mojave.*

were pulled by eighteen mules and two horses. The horses were given the wheel positions because they were both stronger and more obedient than the mules.

Hooked in tandem, the borax wagons each carried a ten-ton load for a total of twenty tons per team. Because the country through which the sweating team labored was among the hottest and driest lands in the world, it was also necessary to attach a 1,200-gallon water wagon to the two wagons carrying the payload. Heavily built with enormous wheels, the borax wagons figured in the legendary tales of Death Valley Scotty, and several borax wagons, long since retired, were brought to Washington, D.C., to roll down Pennsylvania Avenue in the inaugural parade of President Woodrow Wilson. Surviving examples of the wagons may still be seen at the museum at Furnace Creek Ranch in Death Valley.

The teams that pulled the ponderous loads of borax were guided by a jerk line. Each mule knew its position, and if number five were put in the place of number three, the displaced mule was likely to put on a wild demonstration of hurt feelings. A mule skinner had to be particularly adept with his whip to control such large and temperamental teams. He could flick a fly off a mule forty feet ahead without stinging the mule. Next to him sat the swamper, often a boy, who was his all-around general helper. It was the swamper's duty to keep a box of rocks handy so that the skinner could toss them at the misbehaving mules that were beyond the reach of his whip.

Oxen and horses continued to pull their share of freight wagons, but mules came into their own on the western roads. Mule and driver were linked together in daily life both on the trail and in the mines, and have been linked together ever since in western song and story. Mules pulled six-car trains in the mines and sometimes became so tame that they shared a miner's lunch, chewing tobacco, and, in one case, his pipe. They are celebrated in the Montana miner's song:

Right: *At Rapid City, South Dakota, teams of powerful oxen pull lumber wagons hooked in tandem. Great quantities of timber were used in the mines and in building construction. The bullwhacker coils his whip in his hand near the lead team as a proud symbol of office.*

Below: *An ox team lies down in the middle of the main street in Lead, South Dakota, a mining town in the Black Hills gold district. A heavy freight wagon down the street is ready to head for the mines in the surrounding mountains. Oxen took their rest when they could. Dependable and steady, they were faithful friends to the bullwhacker who drove them.*

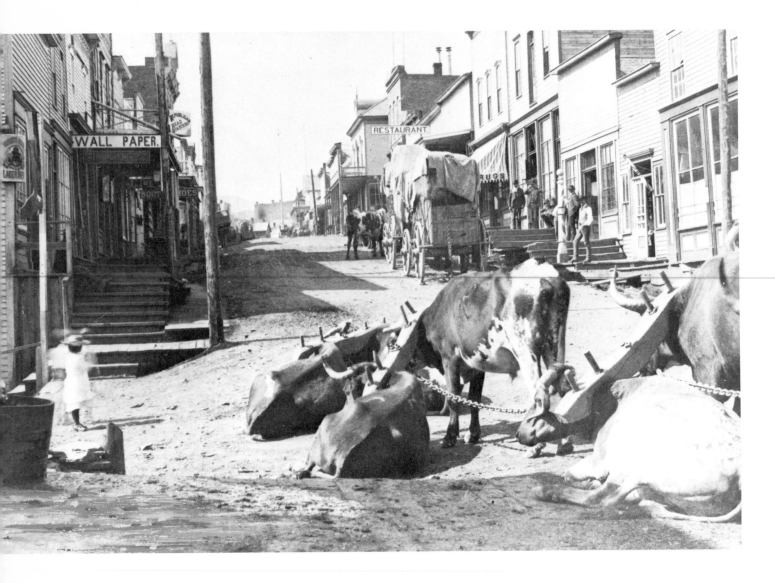

My sweetheart's a mule in the mine.
I drive her with only one line.
On the dashboard I sit
and tobacco I spit,
all over my sweetheart's behind.

Some mule skinners working the freight wagons on the trails were not quite so sure of the affections of their mules. On the Mullan Road a driver literally stripped ribbons of hide off the mules with his whip to get them moving.

"First you've got to get the mule's attention," he explained to a bystander from the East who objected to his whip.

He seared the air with a blast of smoking epithets, and the train got under way. Mule skinners of this persuasion vied with one another in cracking whips. The winner was the one whose whip was the loudest, and this was indeed loud, since the sound could be heard a mile or so away.

It seems that as the frontier grew a little tamer, so did both mules and mule skinners. More and more wagoners discovered that their mules would respond to kindness. Buster Bennington, who hauled limestone in the Mojave Valley, drove ten- and sixteen-mule teams guided by a single line. He controlled his team with two jerks on the line to indicate a right turn and a single jerk to indicate a left turn.

"They were plumb smart," he said of his mules. "They knowed a straight pull every time meant left! Especially when the barns were close."

The better relations between mules and men may have developed because the mules had gained the upper hand. When Bayard Taylor, correspondent for the *New York Tribune,* visited Cheyenne Wells, Colorado, in 1866, he discovered that the mules were living in "a large, handsome frame stable," while the people lived "in a natural cave extending for some thirty feet under the bluff."

Following the collapse of his stable roof under the weight of the snow deposited by the big Cheyenne blizzard of March 7, 1878, freighter Benjamin Smalley moved his furniture from the kitchen to the living room of his house and moved ten mules in.

By all accounts the mule skinners and bull-whackers remained a rough lot, even if they had softened their treatment of both mules and cattle. They were often lousy, in the literal meaning of the word, and would find it necessary to strip naked and throw their garments onto a convenient anthill, where the red ants would devour the lice. They habitually wore red flannel shirts summer and winter, and in Colorado bought jeans that were much too long. This was so they could roll up the cuffs as proof of their prowess. A man who drove a six-mule team wore a six-inch cuff, but an eight-mule driver could turn up his cuffs eight inches.

A teamster's eyes suffered from the glare of the sun. Sir Richard Burton, traveling through the West in 1860, reported that teamsters often wore big green goggles or darkened the skin around their eyes with lampblack to ward off the sun's rays. At night they rolled up in a blanket and slept under their wagons, or on the floor of whatever shelter was handy. They drank any alcohol they could find. Teamsters hauling freight between Drytown and Mokelumne Hill in the California goldfields broke their trip at a certain place. Such a prodigious pile of discarded bottles grew up where they overnighted that the town founded on the site was called Bottileas until more sober folks changed its name to today's Jackson in 1850.

Mule skinners and bullwhackers alike were renowned for their profane tongues, which did not please Alexander Majors of Russell, Majors & Waddell. He made each man carry a Bible and take an oath never to work on Sunday, drink, or swear. The oath ran: "While I am in the employ of Russell, Majors & Waddell, I agree not to use profane language, not to get drunk, not to gamble, not to treat animals cruelly, and not to do anything else that is incompatible with the conduct of a gentleman."

Drivers found this oath hard to live up to. Once another partner, William Waddell, caught a bullwhacker swearing at a team that was straining to pull a wagon out of a mudhole. Waddell remonstrated.

"Boss," said the bullwhacker, "the trouble with them oxen is that they don't understand the kind of language we're talkin' to 'em. Plain 'gee' and 'haw' ain't enough under the present circumstances. Now, if you could jest find it convenient to go off on that thar hill, somewhere, so's you couldn't hear what was goin' on, I'd undertake to get them oxen out."

When Waddell walked away, the driver soon got the team unstuck.

There were not many lady bullwhackers or mule skinners, but those women who did master the trade could hold their own with any males when it came to old-fashioned cussing. Madame Canutson, who drove ten yoke of oxen between Deadwood and Pierre, South Dakota, took care of her year-old baby while her husband worked their homestead, and could earn the proper respect of an ox at the first blaze of her tongue.

Doubtless the most famous feminine teamster was Calamity Jane. Her prowess with a whip is

illustrated in a story that appeared in the *Cheyenne Daily Leader* on July 7, 1877. According to the newspaper account, Calamity Jane invaded the office of the *Cheyenne Daily Leader* and cracked her whip at a big fly on the ceiling over the head of the editor, who had offended her by printing a barbed remark about her reputation. The fly fell to the floor as the editor leaped onto his desk in terror, sprang through the skylight, and hid. She ransacked the place and left a note:

"Print in the *Leader* that Calamity Jane, the child of the regiment and the pioneer white woman of the Black Hills, is in Cheyenne, or I'll scalp you, skin you alive and hang you to a telegraph pole. You hear me, and don't you forget it."

The *Leader* concluded the story with the laconic remark, "There is a vacant chair in our sanctum. The city editor has gone to Borneo."

Rough as a teamster might be, he usually had a soft place in his heart for children, probably because the scarcity of women in the West made it hard for him to marry and raise a family of his own. Boys worked the wagon trains not only as swampers but also as extra hands. In Butte, Montana, it was traditional that in the spring the horses that pulled the ore wagons would have their heavy winter coats clipped short by air-driven hand clippers. Town boys pumped the bellows that supplied the air, and for their pains were given a shearing with the clippers as soon as the men finished with the horses.

A twelve-year-old wild colt named Bill Cody was an extra hand on Lew Simpson's train. Most of the bullwhackers made something of a pet of him, but not one bully, who badgered him night and day. Fortunately for Cody he had made a friend of a lanky young man named Bill Hickok, Ca-lamity's future friend, who was also a teamster with the train. One night at dinner the bully asked the boy to run an errand for him.

"I did not start at once," remembered Cody in his adult years, "and he gave me a slap in the face with the back of his hand, knocking me off an ox-yoke on which I was sitting, and sending me sprawling on the ground. Jumping to my feet, I picked up a camp kettle full of boiling coffee which was setting on the fire, and threw it at him. I hit him in the face, and the hot coffee gave him a severe scalding. He sprang for me with the ferocity of a tiger, and would undoubtedly have torn me to pieces, had it not been for the timely interference of my new-found friend, Wild Bill, who knocked the man down."

Left: *Calamity Jane was a freighter on the Deadwood and Cheyenne trails. She rarely looked as well decked out as in this picture. Calamity Jane could outshoot and outcuss almost any man, and with a crack of her whip she could drop a fly from the ceiling or snap a team into action.*

Below: *Madame Canutson, the "Lady Bullwhacker," could also crack a whip with the best of the men and match them oath for oath. Brandishing her whip, she poses here before a string of wagons traveling on the Deadwood Trail into Dakota Territory.*

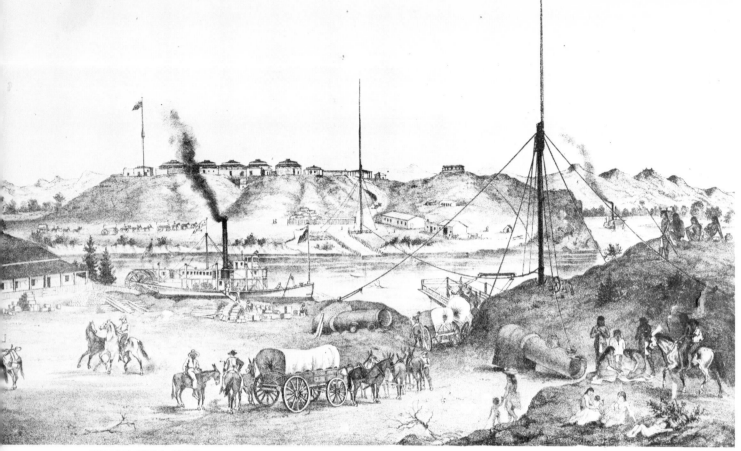

Above: *Fort Yuma, built where the Butterfield Trail crossed the Colorado River, was a key transportation point. Steamers ascended the Colorado from the Gulf of California to land freight, which heavy wagons took west into California or east to New Mexico and Texas.*

Right: *A jaunty team of horses pulled the water wagon at Silverton, Colorado, in 1887. The appearance of a photographer meant that every man available jumped aboard to take a ride.*

When the bully had picked himself up off the ground, he demanded of Wild Bill what business it was of his that he should "put in his oar."

"It's my business to protect that boy, or anybody else, from being unmercifully abused, kicked and cuffed, and I'll whip any man who tries it on!" said Wild Bill. "And if you even lay a hand on that boy—little Billy there—I'll give you such a pounding that you won't get over it for a month of Sundays." This was before Wild Bill took to using a six-gun on people he did not like.

The wagon master, or wagon boss, usually rode at the head of a freight train, and the assistant wagon boss brought up the rear. There might be twenty-five wagons in the caravan, with a twenty-sixth wagon loaded with camp equipment and supplies to be used by the teamsters. The last wagon was usually this mess or kitchen wagon, and it contained not only provisions but cooking utensils, jacks and levers for raising loads, extra tires, rope coils, pulleys, extra wheels and spokes, bars of iron, and even a forge.

"There were thirty-one men all told in a train," wrote Buffalo Bill. "The men did their own cooking, being divided into messes of seven. One man cooked, another brought wood and water, another stood guard, and so on, each having some duty to perform while getting meals."

On some larger trains a managing clerk also went along. In 1866 Thomas Alfred Creigh was managing clerk with a freight train of fifty-two wagons taking eighty-one tons of boilers and quartz-

stamping machinery from Nebraska City to Alder Gulch. He had a special wagon fitted up. It was called the "Reading Room" because it contained a library. There was also an arsenal of rifles, revolvers, and pistols, and a violin to while away the evenings around the campfire. A three-foot U.S. flag flew from the bow of the wagon.

A bull train would move one or two miles in the morning and then pause to allow the animals to rest and urinate. Then it would go on another seven to ten miles before stopping for a second break. While the men ate their breakfast, the animals would graze for a couple of hours. At the end of another seven to ten miles, or three or four hours, the train would stop for supper. After supper the company would move on until dark. In this way

something like twenty miles could be covered in a day. When the wagons were empty, bull teams could go two or three miles farther in a day than when the wagons were loaded.

The wagons built by Joseph Murphy in Saint Louis continued to be popular in freight trains, but as the years passed, more and more freighters turned to Studebaker wagons. Young John Studebaker had reached Placerville, California, with a wagon train, but he never did find time to dig for gold. He was too busy making "Irish baby buggies," as miners called wheelbarrows. At Placerville he began to construct big Washoe wagons of hickory, ash, and wrought iron. The wagons were equipped with powerful brakes and had a stronger and heavier frame and box than wagons made in the East, because

Studebaker was familiar with the rugged conditions to be encountered on the mountain road between Placerville and Virginia City where the wagons were to be used. It proved too difficult to obtain well-seasoned wood in California, so Studebaker moved back to South Bend, Indiana, where plenty of hardwoods were available.

Studebaker fashioned his axles of black hickory and made his skeins of steel. He boiled the running gear in oil to drive out any lingering moisture and to add toughness. He made wagons ranging from one capable of hauling 2,000 pounds to the huge Carson wagon—the Washoe wagon with refinements—which could hold 20,000 pounds and negotiate the mountain roads of California and Nevada. Soon the majority of the wagons encountered on roads in the California-Nevada country were Studebakers, with enormous square boxes and canvas tops. Twelve yoke of oxen pulled the large lead vehicle and the two shorter ones attached to it.

The only western wagonmaker whose freight wagons compared to those made by Studebaker and Murphy was a native of Prussia named Herman Haas, who created the Bain wagon at Cheyenne for particular use in the Wyoming and Black Hills camp trade. In 1876 he advertised that his wagons had "felloes boiled in oil; timber lies in stock years before being used; no tire can come loose in any climate. Every wagon is warranted to be No. One in every respect."

Haas carried a full line of express and freight wagons, and made repairs in his shops. The wagons that he designed for long mountain hauls had the linchpin dropped through the groove in the outer rim of the hub into a rectangular hole in the spindle. This ingenious device held the wheel in place, since the turning wheel kept the pinhead from working out. He also invented wagon shoes that would prevent a vehicle from skidding over a cliff on an icy road. Sharp steel calks hung from a chain that was pinned to the uphill hind wheel.

In the winter teamsters sometimes removed the wheels and replaced them with runners in order to travel over snow-clogged roads. They equipped their animals' hoofs with calks to keep them from falling on the ice.

Winter or summer, wagon masters in the northern Rockies had their troubles with wagons tipping

Left: John Studebaker, blacksmith and wheelwright, settled near Ashland, Ohio, in 1835. There he raised his five sons, who later were to establish a wagon-building shop in South Bend, Indiana, that in time became the largest wagon-manufacturing plant in the world.

Below: Freighters take a meal break beside the trail through Colorado's Berthoud Pass. A freighter was a redoubtable fellow, self-sufficient and skilled at getting along in the wilderness.

over on the steep side slopes over which the rough roads ran. To avoid this the men switched the big hind wheel on the uphill side with the little front wheel on the downhill side. There was far less chance that the wagon would topple with both the big wheels on the downhill slope. When they were on a level stretch of the road, they switched the wheels back again. One thing was certain. On the rocky roads that snaked through the mountains, even the sturdiest of wagons rarely lasted for more than three years.

Some freighters, particularly in Texas, preferred wagons that rocked from side to side. They loaded them to produce this swaying ride because they claimed that carrying the weight on two wheels at a time lightened the drag on the mules. There were wagons with narrow tires which the teamsters called "butcher-knife" wagons, because the tires cut deep, narrow ruts the way a butcher knife would.

Oxen, horses, and mules continued to draw most of the freight vehicles in the West, but experimenters were still attempting to harness the wind. Wind-wagon Thomas' prairie ship had been smashed beyond use on the prairies, but others in Westport were soon trying to perfect a sailing wagon to cruise to the Pikes Peak goldfields. John Parker put wagonsmith William Wells to work constructing a windwagon. It resembled a float in a circus parade. On a moon-lit night a team of oxen hauled it out on the prairie, where it blew away in a strong wind and was never seen again.

This didn't discourage August Rodert, a Westport storekeeper, who erected a windmill similar to those of his native Holland on the bed of an old prairie schooner. When the wind spun the mill, it operated a rawhide belt that turned the rear axle. The wagon moved, but it proved too insubstantial for high plains trips.

Samuel Peppard of Oskaloosa, Kansas, also built a windwagon for the Colorado trade. In 1860 he took a 350-pound light wagon, erected a nine-by-eleven-foot sail over the center of the front axle, and set out across the plains. Steve Randall, J. T. Forbes, and Sid Coldon rode in the wagon with him, along with 400 pounds of supplies and ammunition.

"Our best time was two miles in four minutes," Peppard said later. "One day we went fifty miles in three hours and in doing so passed 625 teams."

Above: "Windwagon" Thomas sailed a windwagon on the plains during the heydey of the Santa Fe trade. His prairie ship ran amok and was smashed beyond use, but this did not keep others in Westport, Missouri, from building windwagons to sail to the Pikes Peak goldfields. Samuel Peppard of Oskaloosa, Kansas, also built a windwagon for the Colorado trade. Carrying 400 pounds of supplies and ammunition in the wagon, a crew sailed off with Peppard, bound for Denver. As they winged by plodding ox teams pulling freight wagons, they joked and gibed. They frightened horses and mules. Then, only fifty miles short of their destination, a whirlwind whipped the machine fifty feet into the air and hurled it to the ground. The rear wheels were broken, and the windwagoners had to beg a ride from a passing freight wagon.

Left: Oxen pulled freight wagons through river crossings. Sometimes a wagon mired in the mud or quicksand. When an ox lost its footing on the slippery bottom of a river or stepped into a deep water hole, the animal would bawl in terror until it had floundered back on its feet.

The dry-land sailors joked with teamsters as they went winging by. Then, only fifty miles northeast of Denver, a whirlwind picked up the machine and flung it fifty feet into the air before dropping it to the ground. The rear wheels were splintered, and the windwagon's occupants had to beg a ride into town from one of the freight wagons they had so jauntily passed.

Windwagon pioneers were not easily discouraged. At last, on April 18, 1860, the *Rocky Mountain News* reported that a windwagon had sailed into Denver. Three men had piloted it from the Missouri River in twenty days, which equaled the speed of the best horse teams with, as the newspaper pointed out, "but a tithe part of the expense."

While windwagons were sailing across the prairies, steamwagons were being tried out far to the north. Joseph Renshaw Brown of Henderson, Minnesota, was the inventor of the steamwagon. At the age of fourteen he had been a fifer and drummer with Lt. Col. Henry Leavenworth's soldiers. After leaving the Army he had tried his hand at various trades and become wealthy.

On July 4, 1859, the citizens of Henderson were treated to their first glimpse of what Brown's money could buy. He had designed a huge and wonderful machine, which he claimed would revolutionize western freighting. The steamwagon possessed red drive wheels twelve feet in diameter. The cleated rims were two feet across. Inside each wheel, gear wheels meshed with the engine. The front wheels were half as high as the rear wheels, and they were geared to the steering wheel, which Brown now held in his firm hands. There was a bright red roof that sparkled in the sunlight, and above everything a stack as high as the town's second-story windows belched black woodsmoke.

Hitching the engine to two carts, each twenty feet long, Brown trundled up and down unpaved Main Street. Brave men and boys accepted his invitation to climb aboard for a rumble out into the countryside. The machine reversed gears and backed up just as smoothly as it had gone ahead. A week later Brown drove his machine to Fort Ridgely at an average speed of eight miles per hour, and climbed a grade of 1,000 feet per mile.

The *Henderson Democrat*, a newspaper which Brown also owned, stated it was "highly gratified with the conviction that the ponderous body possessed the power of locomotion."

Shortly afterwards the "ponderous body" sank in a swamp that Brown had unwisely tried to cross. A party of uncooperative Sioux happened along and shot it full of holes, but Brown was not dismayed. He was now ready to build a new steamwagon—to be called the Prairie Motor—and take it out onto the Nebraska plains, where it would prove its worth.

Brown evidently meant what he said, for on July 19, 1862, the *Nebraska City News* reported:

"Very much to the agreeable surprise of the citizens of this place, the *West Wind* has landed at our levee, on Monday morning last, the first locomotive engine, which ever pressed the soil of Nebraska. It is the Prairie Motor designed for the transportation of passengers and goods over ordinary roads.

"We have no doubt of the ultimate success of the experiment," announced the editor of the *News*.

Brown's new machine had been built by John A. Reed in New York City. It had four engines of ten horsepower each. Its oscillating cylinders connected to a shaft that gave motion to wheels six

Left: *San Francisco was at the western end of the Butterfield Trail. In 1850 wagons and carts rolled down the principal street of the growing city by the Golden Gate. From San Francisco wagons and coaches took the bumpy roads to the goldfields.*

Below: *Front Street in Sacramento, California, was the great entrepôt, or transshipment point, of the West in 1850. Boats ascended the Sacramento River to dock beside the street, and wagons carried freight over the precipitous roads to the mining camps of the Mother Lode.*

feet in diameter. These were attached to the inner spokes of the ten-foot-high drive wheels. The drive wheels, made of boiler iron, had an eighteen-inch tread. The front steering wheels were six feet in diameter and were attached to the steering mechanism by a ball and socket arrangement.

A tank formed the body of the steamwagon. An upright boiler stood aft of the drive shaft. The machine could carry enough wood and water for four hours, an engineer, a fireman, and a pilot.

The *News* was not alone in its excitement; everybody else was excited too. The steamwagon rolled off the *West Wind* under its own power and climbed up the road leading from the levee, where today a rest stop put in by the local Lions Club provides a scenic overlook. Unfortunately the boiler had been filled with muddy Missouri River water, and the cylinders worked badly. Brown had to have the engine cleaned out before he could make the first trial run.

At last everything was ready. The steamwagon triumphantly climbed Kearny Heights, crossed Table Creek at Rock Ford in a drizzling rain, sank its heavy wheels six inches into a settler's newly plowed field, and crashed through thickets of hazel and sumac. When it came clanking and hissing back into town, boys ran after it shouting.

The women of the town got into a freight wagon for a ride behind the steamwagon. They stood up and held on to the side of the wagon for dear life. Judge David Goff put on his new straw hat and rode with them. He did not even seem to mind when a spark flew back from the engine and set his hat on fire. The day was a great success.

Brown sent men ahead to cut wood on the prairies along the proposed route to Denver, so that the steamwagon would have plenty of fuel available. He hitched up several freight wagons behind the machine and set out for the goldfields. On August 2 the *News* printed word of his steamwagon's fate:

"Gen. Brown's steamwagon, which left here last week, has, we regret to learn, met with an obstruction in the shape of an accident. About twelve miles from the city one of the cranks of the driving shaft broke and stopped further progress for the present. On an examination it was discovered that the breakage was caused by an original flaw so concealed that it could not be suspected."

On August 30 a new crank was sent out from New York City, but the machine never resumed its journey west. The Sioux had attacked Brown's home in Minnesota and killed most of his family. Stricken by grief, the inventor hurried home. He would return some day, people of Nebraska City were certain, and he would fix his steamwagon and continue his trip across the plains. Nebraskans built a road with tax money as far as the abandoned steamwagon, and to this day it is called Steamwagon Road.

We drove out Steamwagon Road in the summertime of 1976, when the corn was laughing in the wind. The road passes an abandoned schoolhouse and comes to a monument close to a mailbox with the name of farmer Sauberzweig on it. In Sauberzweig's field, 100 feet to the northwest, is the exact spot where the Prairie Motor stopped for good. The monument was unveiled on October 30, 1914, by Mrs. Edmond E. Woolsey, then seventy-six years old, who had ridden aboard the freight wagon behind the smoke-belching steamwagon on that proud day when it seemed that the Prairie Motor would span the plains.

The steamwagon was finally dragged to Arbor Lodge, the Nebraska City home of Julius Sterling Morton, founder of Arbor Day. Jim Carney, assistant superintendent of the Arbor Lodge State Park, told the Otoe County Historical Society, "It stood for many years as a monument, very convenient for children to play on and for bees to nest in, and it was finally broken up for old iron, though parts of its machinery went into the Nebraska City Gas Works."

Brown died in a New York City hotel in 1870. At the time of his death he was still trying to build a new steamwagon that would revolutionize transportation on the high plains. In the Appendix to his novel *The God-Seeker* Sinclair Lewis said of his fellow Minnesotan, "Perhaps as much as anyone he was the inventor of the automobile."

Following the demise of the Prairie Motor, the western trails were left to freight wagons pulled by draft animals. Heavy wagons at costs averaging from six to ten cents a pound, but sometimes as high as twenty cents or even forty cents, brought freight from the Missouri to Denver. For shorter distances the charge depended on which kind of freight service was used. Corn freight, employing horses or mules, was faster but more costly than grass freight, employing oxen. By carrying corn for feed the freighter could speed up his trip, but less freight could be carried because the corn took up space. A slower ox team feeding on the prairie grass could pull more freight. It was logical that heavy freight and goods that did not need fast transport would be sent by grass freight, but people paid a premium for

Horses and mules provided corn freight and oxen provided grass freight. Corn freight was faster but more expensive, since corn carried aboard the wagons for feeding the horses or mules left less space for freight. Oxen did not require any storage space for their fodder; they received adequate nourishment from the prairie grass. Mining towns paid a premium rate to speed vital equipment and such perishables as butter and eggs by corn freight.

corn freight to speed the delivery of butter, eggs, dressed hogs, sausages, and other perishables.

Big freight companies carried much of the cargo. They went almost—but not quite—everywhere, as the following anecdote illustrates. A bullwhacker walked into Majors' office to ask for a job.

"Can you drive oxen?" demanded Majors.

"Yep, I can drive oxen to hell and back."

"Well, well. I can't use you because our firm doesn't make that point."

It was just about the only point that Russell, Majors & Waddell did not make.

At the same time there were thousands of "shotgun" freighters, independent teamsters who drove their own wagons. Shotgun freighters were a colorful lot. Ordinarily they bought supplies at railhead or at a river town and hauled them to a remote point where they could be sold at a tidy profit.

Alexander Toponce was a small freighter. While driving through Brigham City, Utah, on his way back to the Montana goldfields, he saw a dressed hog hanging in a store. He paid thirty-six dollars for the 600-pound porker.

"There was no place in my wagon for it," he said later, "so I got three men to help me, and I put it right up on the top over the wagon cover, all spread out on top of the wagon bows, with his snout pointing towards Montana, and with a rope tied

Left: Crude guardrails were erected to keep the freight wagons on the rough roads that zigzagged over Colorado's Continental Divide.

Below: Draft animals hauled the heavy machinery into place in early mining operations at the Colorado goldfields.

to each leg and fastened down to the wagon bed. The carcass was already frozen and stayed frozen all the way to Montana."

On Christmas Eve, 1863, Toponce and his pig rolled into Virginia City.

"I stopped in front of Alex Metzel's butcher shop," he wrote, "and Alex offered me a dollar a pound for the pig, which I accepted in gold dust and reserved six pounds of the best chops for our supper."

Two freighters loaded their wagon with frozen oysters at the Missouri River and hauled them to Colorado, where they sold them at two dollars and fifty cents a quart. Other freighters carried a load of apples to Denver, where they brought fifteen dollars a bushel. A wagonload of cats was also brought to Denver, and the cats were disposed of as mousers at a tidy profit.

Perhaps Phatty Thompson, a shotgun freighter who drove between Cheyenne and Deadwood, learned of the Colorado freighter's success with cats. He presented a cat to a dance-hall girl in Deadwood. The cat was a champion mouser and an endearing pet, particularly since he gave a certain authentic feline atmosphere to an abode that some of the miners referred to as a cathouse.

On his next trip to Cheyenne, Phatty paid kids twenty-five cents per cat for all the cats they could bring him. There were to be no questions asked, and both homeless alley cats and the pampered pets of many a Cheyenne family disappeared into Phatty's wagon. A German brewer descended on Phatty before he could pull out of town and accused him of stealing his cat. Phatty denied his guilt at great length, but finally had to surrender the brewer's puss.

As Phatty and his wagonload of cats crossed Spring Creek near Hill City in the Black Hills, the wagon upset. Eighty-two caterwauling cats escaped. Phatty put out food for the cats and lured all but one back into captivity. Some passing miners helped him to capture the holdout.

Above: *The California Trail snaked through the Sierra Nevadas. By 1865 the trail had become the main road from the Mother Lode country across the mountains to the Nevada mining camps. Stagecoaches, wagons, and carts were all part of the jumble of traffic that followed the road, when winter's furious snows did not block the pass.*

Right, top: *When the country was so rough that wheels could roll no farther, pack stock took up the burdens. Burros were used to carry lumber from Ouray, Colorado, to the mines.*

Right, bottom: *A train of freight wagons reached Del Norte, Colorado, in 1877 with supplies and equipment for the mines.*

When he reached Deadwood, Phatty parked his wagon on lower Main Street and sold the cats at from ten to twenty-five dollars apiece. Many took up feline domesticity in the cathouses on upper Main Street. One sextet of tomcats was even said to sit on a backyard fence and yodel in a way to make a Swiss jealous. Phatty, claim old Deadwood wags, had trained them on Swiss cheese.

Freight wagons carried almost everything to the mining camps. The big Murphy or Studebaker might haul a box of books, a piano, nails, window glass, boilers, or lace parasols, but above all it carried provisions. One day a freight wagon arrived at Deadwood with a load of twenty barrels of whiskey and one sack of flour.

"What do they want with all that flour?" asked one of the miners as he inspected the cargo.

After a cruel winter such a jest turned sour. When the first supply train of the season reached Virginia City, Montana, on May 22, 1864, the entire town lined the street to cheer its entry into town. To reach mining camps isolated by the heavy mountain snows, mule skinners and bullwhackers braved winter blizzards. When the snow grew so deep that they could not get their teams through without lightening the load, teamsters hefted huge sacks of flour on their backs and carried them. They reloaded beyond the deepest drifts, and the wagons continued on their way. When the wagons reached the lonely and half-starved town at the end of the wintry road, women and children cried with relief. Vital transportation in the mining West rolled on wagon wheels.

Above: *When freight teams left Cimarron, New Mexico, to haul machinery to
the Elizabethan Gold Mines, two pioneer boys turned out—one of them wheel-
ing his bicycle—to see the stirring sight, but the presence of a photographer
stole their attention from the wagons.*

Left: *Strings of ore wagons carry the precious minerals from a Nevada mine.
Each wagon has a brakeman to slow the heavy vehicle's progress down the steep
inclines along the way.*

Above: *A freighter's "mobile home" might be attached to the rear of his string of wagons and a farm implement might roll on its own wheels to its purchaser, as in this Chinook, Montana, scene.*

Right: *An empty ore wagon on its way to the Chamberlain Mine shaft at Idaho Springs, Colorado, in the 1870s passes full wagons heading in the other direction.*

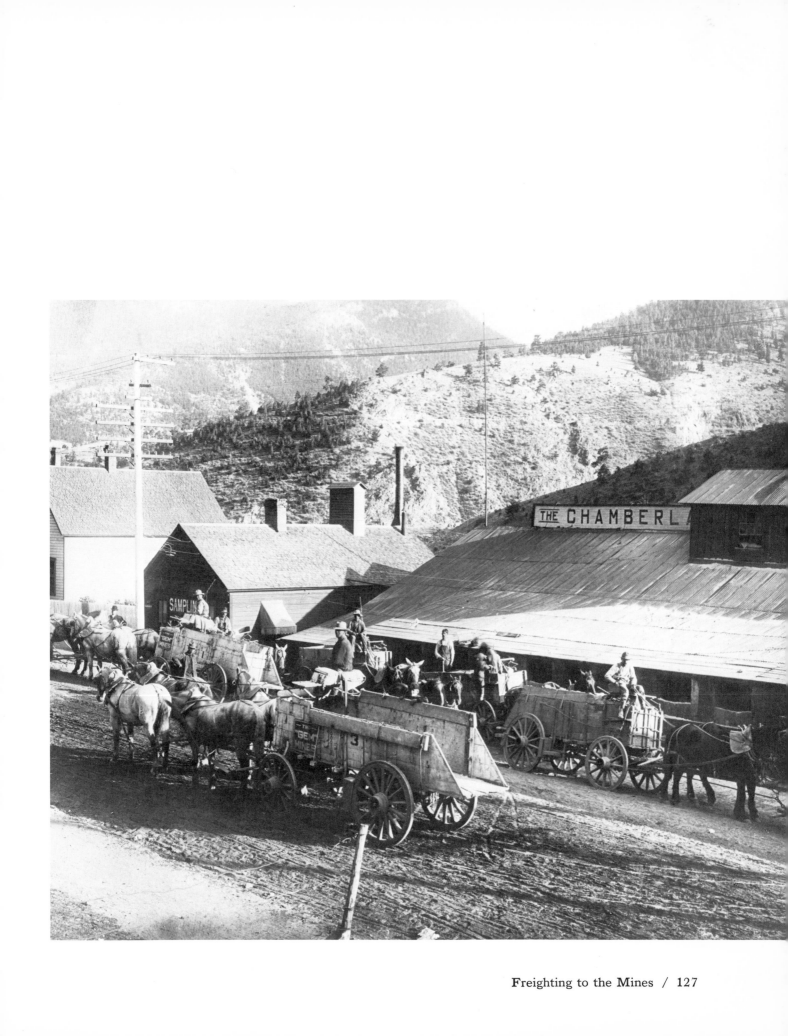

On June 20, 1868, a wagon train belonging to David Bruce Powers of Leavenworth, Kansas, circled dramatically to impress local citizens on Denver's Holladay Street. Later the mules were lost in an Indian raid south of Denver.

WILDERNESS "EXPRESS"-THE STAGECOACHES

THERE WERE three classes of stagecoach service in the Old West. Let the horses come to a steep hill, and the driver shouted, "First class passengers, stay where you are; second class passengers, get out and walk, and third class passengers, get out and push!"

In 1877 the *Omaha Herald* printed an article called "Hints for Plains Travelers":

The best seat inside a stage coach is the one next the driver. . . . If a team runs away, sit still and take your chances; if you jump, nine times out of ten you will be hurt. . . . Don't smoke a strong pipe inside especially early in the morning, spit on the leeward side of the coach. . . . Don't swear, nor lop over on your neighbor when sleeping. . . . Never attempt to fire a gun or pistol while on the road; it may frighten the team. . . . Don't discuss politics or religion. . . . Don't grease your hair before starting or dust will stick there in sufficient quantities to make a respectable "tater" patch. . . .

The article also advises that a person shouldn't wear tight-fitting boots, shoes, or gloves, and if the driver asks him to get out and walk, he should do so without complaining. If the weather turns cold, he must not drink hard liquor or he will freeze.

To most twentieth-century Americans a frontier stagecoach was bound to be a Concord, but this was not the case. It might be anything from a renovated French omnibus—the first vehicle carrying passengers from San Francisco to San Jose—to a sturdy coach made in Cheyenne by the Cheyenne Carriage Works for the Black Hills, or a Troy coach built in Troy, New York. It might be a Jersey wagon or a dearborn fixed up for the purpose, a jerky, a mud wagon, a sand wagon, or a celerity wagon. If it carried the mail, express, and passengers, it was called a stage regardless of what kind of vehicle it was.

One of the earliest stage lines to operate beyond the wide Missouri took passengers over the Santa Fe Trail between Independence and Santa Fe. The first coach left Independence in May, 1846. A writer in the *Missouri Commonwealth*, published in Independence, reported: "The stages are gotten up in elegant style and are each arranged to convey eight passengers. The bodies are beautifully painted and made water tight with a view of using them as boats in ferrying streams."

The Mahaffie depot in Olathe, Kansas, is much the same today as when it was the first stop out of Independence. The coaches pulled by six-mule teams rattled up to the depot, where passengers could get out and stretch their legs. They had paid $150 for the trip to Santa Fe. Their fare granted them the right to bring along forty-five pounds of baggage and to eat and sleep on the ground.

In *The Southwestern Frontier* Carl Coke Rister quotes a man who traveled by stagecoach from San Francisco to Tipton, Missouri:

"Twenty-four mortal days and nights—twenty-five being schedule time—must be spent in that ambulance; passengers becoming crazy with whisky, mixed with want of sleep, are often obliged to be strapped to their seats; their meals, dispatched during their ten minute halts, are simply abominable, the heats are excessive, the climate malarious; lamps may not be used at nights for fear of non-existent Indians."

Above: *Mud wagons of Butterfield's Overland Mail Company jolted over the roads between Tipton, Missouri, and San Francisco, carrying passengers and mail.*

Right: *Butterfield's Overland Mail eastbound from San Francisco started with a flourish, but once the passengers were well out of town their handsome Concord was exchanged for a utilitarian mud wagon that could negotiate the rugged roads and trails with greater success.*

It was not at all certain that Indians were non-existent. When passengers got too uproarious, the driver shouted, "Indians!" That was certain to quiet them down. If a man cursed too much or showed disrespect to a woman passenger, he was set afoot.

The coach that was so glowingly described by the *Missouri Commonwealth* writer was a spring wagon with seats and canvas top. Three wagons traveled together. One was for the mail and baggage, one for feed, water, and provisions, and one for passengers. At night the wagons were placed in a triangle for defense against an attack by the "non-existent" Indians.

In the fall of 1849 John Whistman refurbished his French omnibus to begin service out of San Francisco. That same autumn twenty-one-year-old James Birch, who had crossed the plains with an ox team, fixed up a springless farm wagon with boards as seats and offered regular service from Sacramento to the gold diggings. He charged $32, and he carried so many people that he soon was importing horses from Australia for as much as $1,000 apiece to take the place of the four western mustangs that pulled his first stage. As the years passed, Birch and other operators made Sacramento the hub of stage lines in northern California.

June 24, 1850, was a proud day for California staging, because on that date the first Concord coach shipped around the Horn by clipper arrived in San Francisco. With its landscape-adorned panels and damask-lined curtains it seemed the last word in luxurious and comfortable transportation. Over the next few decades Concords put in their appearance all over the West, and to miners, gamblers, gunfighters, soldiers on leave, ranchers and cowpunchers, ladies of dubious reputation and just plain ladies—the broad spectrum of frontier humanity—they represented the way to go.

To most western Americans the Concord coach, with its brilliant red, vermilion, yellow, black, or green paint, was a thing of beauty, but to Sir Richard Burton, who rode one to Salt Lake City in 1860, its bold color caused the "antelopes to stand and stretch their large eyes whenever the vehicle comes in sight." (Burton's interpretation of the antelopes' behavior may well be mistaken, however, for the antelope, like most other hoofed mammals, probably cannot perceive colors.)

Burton further remarked about the Concord coach, "It is built to combine safety, strength, and lightness, without the slightest regard to appearances."

The wheels of the coach Burton rode in were set five to six feet apart, affording security against upsets. The larger wheels of his coach had fourteen spokes and seven felloes, and the smaller twelve spokes and six felloes.

"The tyres are of unusual thickness, and polished like steel by the hard dry ground," he wrote, "and the hubs or naves and the metal nave-bands are in massive proportions."

The wagon bed was supported by iron bands, or perpendiculars, abutting upon wooden rockers, which in turn rested on strong leather thoroughbraces. The thoroughbraces not only broke jolts better than steel springs, but could also be repaired in the field. The top was covered by waterproof duck supported by stiff bars of white oak. There was a sunshade in front where the driver sat, a curtain behind him that could be raised or lowered, and four flaps on each side that could be either folded up or fastened down with hooks and eyes.

Burton continued with his detailed description of the Concord coach:

In front sits the driver with usually a conductor or passenger by his side; a variety of packages, large and small, is stowed away under his leather cushion; when the break must be put on, an operation often involving the safety of the vehicle, his right foot is planted upon an iron bar which presses by a leverage upon the rear wheels,—and in hot weather a bucket for watering the animals hangs over one of the lamps, whose companion is usually found wanting. The inside has either two or three benches fronting to the fore or placed *vis-à-vis;* they are moveable and reversible, with leather cushions and hinged padded backs; unstrapped and turned down they convert the vehicle into a tolerable bed for two persons or two and a half.

Mailbags were supposed to be stowed under the seats, or placed where the passengers could perch on top of them. But usually the driver crammed the bags between the wagon bed and the platform, so that, according to Burton, "when ford-waters wash the hubs, the letters are pretty certain to endure ablution."

Burton obviously would not have agreed with the breed of frontiersmen who considered the Concord stage too comfortable, and therefore effeminate and injurious to the health.

The story of the legendary Concords begins in New England in 1813, when Lewis Downing, who had grown up in a family carriage business at Lexington, Massachusetts, opened a wheelwright shop in Concord, New Hampshire. He began with sixty dollars in savings and a few tools. On November 8, 1813, he sold his first rig to Benjamin Kimball, a relative. In 1816 he erected a small factory to build freight wagons and two-wheeled chaises. He employed twelve journeymen and apprentices, and in 1826 he hired a twenty-two-year-old journeyman named J. Stephens Abbot, a chaise builder from Salem, Massachusetts, who became his partner in January of 1828.

Downing's father-in-law was a stage driver, and it came naturally that Downing and Abbot should design a stagecoach. English stagecoaches were not only heavy, but top-heavy, so that they turned over easily on rough American roads. It was up to Abbot to shape the tops of the coaches, and he followed the prevailing style of a modified oval body that derived its strength from the principle of the egg. The panels were curved at the sides, but the ends

Above: *This rare photo of a Nott Line stage crossing the Continental Divide in Colorado is one of a very few showing a frontier stage in motion. Working with cumbersome cameras and tricky wet plates, a photographer found it almost impossible to take such an action picture.*

Left: *A splendidly preserved Concord stage is kept in a park at Spearfish, South Dakota, to remind twentieth-century citizens of the first vehicles to link their community with the outside world.*

were kept wide enough for three passengers to sit side by side in each of the three seats. The rounded top allowed quick drainage. Later the rounded top was straightened. An iron railing at the back and on both sides made it possible to strap excess baggage there. The driver's seat was raised to give a better view of the road ahead, better control of the horses or mules, and more leverage when applying the brakes.

"Honesty, industry, perseverance and economy will secure any person with ordinary health a good living and something for a rainy day," said Downing. The firm conducted its business on this basis. Downing insisted on the best craftsmanship and the use

of only the finest materials. He designed spokes and felloes of great strength. Each spoke was given the same exact shape and weight as each other spoke to ensure correct balance. They were mortised into the hub so tightly that they could not be pulled out. The felloes were band-sawed to a precise arc, width, and thickness, and were also perfectly balanced as to weight. Downing dished his wheels inward with cunning so that they would defy centrifugal force as the vehicle sped around corners. The wood he used had been dried and sun-warped in each direction for three years so that it would not shrink in the arid West. White oak was used for the spokes, and elm or black cherry for the hubs. Basswood was considered appropriate for the panels and roof, but the body frame, felloes, pole, axle beds, and perches were fashioned from white ash. Wood varieties were carefully selected to fit the peculiar requirements of each part of the coach.

Hand-forged iron from Norway was used in making not only the axles and bearings, but also the door handles, hinges, angle irons, and bracings. Norwegian iron combined strength and lightness.

The steel springs of English coaches were not only springless, but they snapped under rough use, particularly in subfreezing weather. Downing overcame this problem by replacing the springs with leather thoroughbraces, which were long strips of steerhide that held up the body of the coach and absorbed the jolts in the road. As much as three to four inches thick, these straps stretched from the front to the rear of the frame.

The chassis of a Concord coach was an ingenious device for cushioning passengers from jolts on a rough road. Its manufacturer could claim that no other suspension system was as easy on stage horses like the Concord team shown here.

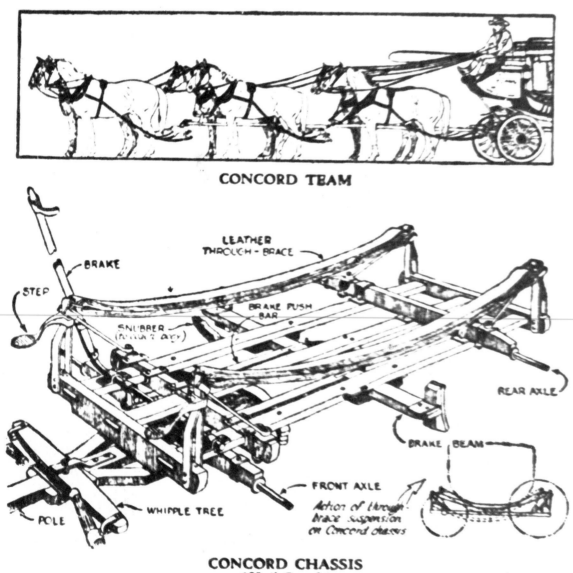

CONCORD TEAM

CONCORD CHASSIS
(Mail Coach)

Supported on thoroughbraces, the coach swung from side to side, but it would not tip over easily. Because its sway was enough to make even Wild Bill Hickok seasick, the Concord was called "Pitching Betsy" in the West. Let a passenger complain, and the driver would assure him that it might disturb the occupants of the stage a bit, but it spared the horses. What's more, thoroughbraces rarely broke. One did break, however, as Mark Twain rode a Concord into the West. In *Roughing It* he describes how the driver dumped half the mail on the prairie and redistributed the rest in order to take the weight off the mended thoroughbrace.

To put a tire on the wheel, the blacksmith heated the tire red-hot to expand its diameter, placed it on the wooden rim, and then dipped it into cold water. The shrinking iron hugged the rim. The brake was a long wooden foot lever on the right-hand side of the driver's seat. It gripped the rear wheels with so much force that it could lock them.

The doors on most coaches came with glass windows. The sash lowered into a pocket between the panels. On each side of the door leather curtains kept out the cold air and a reasonable amount of dust. They could be rolled up in warm weather and attached to straps above the windows.

A Concord's paint job was impressive. Several coats were used, and each was rubbed down with pumice. Over the whole brilliant color the painters carefully applied two coats of spar varnish. Once a Concord coach was carried to the ocean floor in a sinking ship. It stayed in Davy Jones' locker for three months. When it was lifted to the surface, the paint was untouched by the salty deep.

J. Burgum was the staff artist who created the gems of early American art that decorated the doors of the Concord coaches. Each coach had a different picture, which might be a landscape, the portrait of a famous American, or a design. While Burgum was painting the picture, Charles Knowlton was carving the scrollwork, which was painted with gilt. The scrollwork also varied from coach to coach.

Staff artist J. Burgum painted the pictures that decorated the doors of Concord coaches. Each coach had a different picture—perhaps a landscape, the portrait of a famous American, or a design. Charles Knowlton carved the scrollwork of this coach, which is on exhibit at the Museum of Science and Industry in Chicago. The carving was painted with gilt.

Usually a coach was given a name selected by the company that had ordered it. It might be called the "Sacramento" or "Deadwood," indicating a destination, or, more imaginatively, "Prairie Queen," "Star of the North," "Western Monarch," or, surprisingly, "Queen Victoria," "Pocahontas," "Columbus," or "Erin Go Bragh."

Each was invariably given a number, stamped either on the body frame under the driver's seat or under the middle seat of the body and on each axle end. The Abbot and Downing Company kept a careful record of each coach—its purchaser, its destination, and, if possible, where it was resold later in its often long life on the road. The coach in the Serra Museum in San Diego, for example, bears the number 158. The company's records show that this coach was finished in Concord on August 17, 1866. It was first shipped to Edward Herr, a New York City hotel man, and then either brought around the Horn to California or carried west on a railroad flatcar. It operated on various stage lines in California, and fortunately found its way to the museum.

One of the largest orders given to Abbot and Downing—for thirty coaches—came from Wells, Fargo & Company on April 2, 1867. It took Abbot and Downing a year to finish the order. On April 15, 1868, the *Concord Daily Monitor* noted:

A novel sight was presented in the Concord Railroad Yard at noon, Wednesday in the shape of a special train of fifteen platform cars containing thirty elegant coaches from the world-renowned carriage manufactory of Messrs. Abbot, Downing & Co., and four long box cars, containing sixty four-horse sets of harnesses from James J. Hill & Co.'s celebrated harness manufactory, and spare work for repairing the coaches, such as bolts, hubs, spokes, thoroughbraces, etc., all consigned to Wells, Fargo & Co., Omaha and Salt Lake City, the whole valued at $45,000 perhaps. It is the largest lot of coaches ever sent from one manufactory at one time, probably.

The newspaper comments further on the beauty of the red bodies and the yellow running parts, of the scrollwork and the landscape paintings on the doors. Each coach was designed for nine persons inside and eight or ten outside, and usually weighed about 2,250 pounds. The best part of fourteen sides of leather was used to make each coach's thoroughbraces and boots.

When the coaches reached Omaha, they were put into immediate service. By 1876 some of them were rolling between Cheyenne and the Black Hills, and they performed so well that a new operator,

A Wells Fargo & Company treasure box contained the valuables shipped by stage. They were always the prime target of stage robbers.

STAMPEDING WAGON TRAIN HORSES by Frederic Remington

A DOUBTFUL VISITOR by Charles M. Russell

BRUIN NOT BUNNY TURNED THE LEADERS by Charles M. Russell

Above: *The Wells, Fargo & Company Express office still stands in the gold camp town of Columbia, California.*

Below: *On April 15, 1868, a train made up of fifteen platform cars carrying thirty elegant Concord coaches, and four long boxcars containing sixty sets of four-horse harnesses and spare parts for the coaches, such as bolts, hubs, spokes, and thoroughbraces, set out from Concord, New Hampshire, bound for Omaha and Salt Lake City. Wells, Fargo & Company had ordered the coaches from Abbot and Downing a year earlier. The Concord Daily Monitor noted: "It is the largest lot of coaches ever sent from one manufactory at one time, probably."*

Gilmer, Salisbury and Patrick, ordered thirty more to be shipped "with all haste" to Cheyenne.

Ben Holladay's celebrated Overland Stage Company, which together with John Butterfield's Overland Mail Company pioneered in tying together the far-flung western settlements, proved to be another major customer. Holladay ordered luxurious twelve-passenger coaches costing $1,000 apiece. They were pulled by well-matched four- and six-horse teams, and as the line expanded they soon were reaching points in such remote parts of the West that Holladay became legendary. The speed of his Concords was also legendary. In *Roughing It* Twain tells of a nineteen-year-old American who accompanied him on a visit to the Holy Land. An elderly man who was well-versed in the Bible explained that Moses had taken forty years to lead the children of Israel 300 miles.

"Forty years? Only three hundred miles? Humph! Ben Holladay would have fetched them through in thirty-six hours!" exclaimed the young American.

The West was scarcely the only place to encounter a Concord in all its glory. The Palmer House in Chicago ordered magnificent coaches in canary yellow. A firm in Bolivia took delivery on five coaches. It had ordered the company to "ornament up fancy and put women on door panel." A coach "trimmed with purple goatskin inside" was sent to Veracruz, Mexico. Other coaches were shipped to Australia and South Africa, where conditions on the frontier were similar to those in the American West.

In 1847 Abbot and Downing separated, but Downing's son renewed the partnership in 1865. A second generation of Abbots joined the firm. The company brought workmen from England, Scotland, and Canada. These put in twelve- to fourteen-hour days except on Saturday, when six o'clock was quitting time. After the end of the stagecoach era, the company made ambulances, gun carriages, circus wagons, and finally truck bodies and fire engines. In 1928 the firm went out of business, but it left a legacy of American craftsmanship that has survived the frontier.

The quality of the Concord's running gear was unsurpassed. A coach now in the Arbor Lodge collection at Nebraska City, Nebraska, was purchased by Holladay in May, 1862. It ran between Atchison, Kansas, and Denver for a third of a century, but its running gear is still perfect. In addition to exporting complete coaches, Downing and Abbot shipped abroad a vast number of wheels. American wheels became so popular in England that J. Philipson, a British coach authority, complained, "It is difficult to understand why so many American made wheels are used in this country. They are usually well and accurately built, but why should our wheel manufacturers not use similar machinery and produce similar work?"

Butterfield is credited with the design of the first celerity wagon. It had the undercarriage of a Concord, but the top frame was covered with canvas and the entire vehicle was lighter in weight, so that it could fly over the rough roads with greater ease. Waterman Ormsby, a correspondent for the *New York Herald,* rode a celerity wagon on a trip from Missouri to San Francisco.

"Each one has three seats," he wrote, "which are arranged so that the backs let down and form one bed, capable of accommodating from four to ten, according to their size and how they lie. I found it a very agreeable bed for one."

On a trip from the Missouri to the Far West, a passenger might start out in a Concord coach, but after the first stop at a way station he was likely to be transferred to a celerity wagon. He would not see a Concord again until the last stop before his final destination.

The Abbot and Downing Company and other manufacturers also made a lightweight vehicle called a mud wagon. This "poor man's Concord" was inexpensive to make, with flat sides and simpler joinery. The thoroughbraces were not suspended from the standards, but rather were looped over a low crossbar. This gave the vehicle a lower center of gravity than that of the Concord coach, so that it could maneuver over more treacherous roads with impunity. Its flat-bottomed body was attached to a sledlike iron frame. There were no doors or windows. The sides were open to the fresh breezes except in inclement weather, when canvas curtains could be lowered. The vehicle was sturdy enough to take the worst that a western road could offer.

The sand wagon was another specialized vehicle used in the West. It stood high off the ground on wide tires. When a stage reached a river ford that was too deep for it to cross, the passengers were transferred to a sand wagon to make the crossing. Another coach waited on the far bank to take them on their way.

For short distances some stage lines carried their passengers in a jerky, which an Army wife on a trip from Kit Carson, Colorado, to Fort Lyon called "a funny looking stage coach." It was a light,

Above: *An eastern illustrator, Theodore R. Davis, sketched an Overland Mail coach in Guy's Gulch for* Harper's Weekly *while crossing the Colorado Rockies.* Harper's *sent him through the West on an illustrating assignment in 1865.*

Right: *Traveling through the western mountains by stagecoach was an adventurous experience. This stage is on its way to the Colorado mines. The horses are well-matched whites, a sign of first-class service.*

two-seat conveyance with roll-up canvas sides. The jerky was springless, and nobody ever claimed that the ride it gave was smooth.

During the last few decades of the stagecoach era, small western manufacturers made some of the coaches used. Among them was the Cheyenne Carriage Works, which specialized in wagons for pros-

pectors but also turned out such stages as the "Wyoming," the last coach to run to the Black Hills from Cheyenne. A. D. Butler of Cheyenne also contributed to the Wyoming city's reputation as the "Concord of the West." He constructed a "treasure coach" for the Black Hills runs. The interior of this express coach was lined with steel plates five-

sixteenths of an inch thick. Test rifles were fired at the coach from a distance of only fifty feet without penetrating the steel. There were portholes in the doors to allow the men inside to shoot at any road agents who attempted to waylay the stage. The coach was called "The Iron Clad" by some and "The Monitor" by others. It was such a success that a second steel-plated monster named "The Johnny Slaughter" was built and put into service.

Coan and Ten Broeke of Chicago shipped eight new coaches to the Southern Mail and Express Company for use in Colorado, and there were small eastern manufacturers as well. When Butterfield expressed a preference for the Troy coach over the Concord coach itself, this lightweight coach—made at

Troy, New York, by Eaton, Gilbert and Company —enjoyed a reputation as the "new Concord."

Traveling by stagecoach in the Old West was rarely dull. What with Indians, bandits, mud, quicksand, floods, and storms, there was always something to enliven a trip. Perhaps it was the narrowness of a road through forested mountains.

"If you kin see daylight between the trees, you kin get through," said the driver.

Perhaps it was a headlong plunge down a steep hill with the brakes creaking and groaning. If it was an icy or unusually steep hill, the driver and passengers tied a log onto the rear to slow the coach's descent. Perhaps it was overtaking a freighter on a narrow mountain road.

"Clar the road!" shouted the driver. "Get out of the way thar with your bull team!"

Some drivers attached knives to long poles, and as they rocketed by they slashed at the draft animals of a teamster who failed to get out of the way soon enough.

Every part of the West had its road hazards. From Santa Cruz to Pescadero on the California coast stages ran along the beach, where the surf crashed ashore. They could make it over the hard-packed sandy strip at the foot of the cliffs only during low tide. Sometimes there was a race between the stage and the incoming tide. It was enough to shake an unnerved passenger's confidence in the knight of the reins.

In the winter runners often replaced wheels in the snow-laden mountains or on the northern plains. An all-weather stagecoach used at Meeker, Colorado, had wheels in the front and runners in the back so it could keep going all winter long. Often bells were hung from the horses, and they jingled as the horses and stagecoach glided over the packed snow.

Passengers kept warm in the winter with the help of buffalo robes and hot bricks or rocks wrapped in gunnysacks beneath their feet. On some lines foot warmers with live coals in them were used. Passengers in the Black Hills filled their coach with hay, wrapped themselves in fur coats and robes, and slumbered comfortably even at temperatures as low as thirty-five degrees below zero. The whiskers on the driver were calculated to keep him warm enough.

The driver was hailed as a celebrity wherever he went. Twain observes in *Roughing It,* "The stage-driver was a hero—a great and shining dignitary, the world's favorite son, the envy of the people, the observed of the nations. When they spoke to him they received his insolent silence meekly, and as being the natural and proper conduct of so great a man; when he opened his lips they all hung on his words with admiration...."

Henry Ward, a driver, remembered in his old age that "passengers riding on the seat with the drivers was supposed to treat the driver to drinks and cigars on the road."

Each line had its most celebrated drivers, but the most colorful of all seemed to take the reins in California. There was teetotaler Frank Jordan, who could take his stagecoach through any blizzard or bandit attack to safety.

"I don't drink. I won't drink, and I don't like to see anybody else drink," he said. "I'm of the opinion of these mountains—keep your top cool. They've got snow, and I've got brains, that's all the difference."

Above: *Each stage driver dressed to fit his reputation. Mark Twain wrote: "The stage-driver was a hero—a great and shining dignitary, the world's favorite son, the envy of the people, the observed of the nations. When they spoke to him they received his insolent silence meekly, and as being the natural and proper conduct of so great a man; when he opened his lips they all hung on his words with admiration...."*

Right: *Western roads spanned canyons and gushing streams on rickety bridges built by amateur engineers from logs and timbers. A stagecoach swaying over such a bridge was enough to make a brave man turn pale.*

Above: *Charlie Parkhurst could guide his stage at breakneck speed over mountain roads. This illustration shows him before he lost an eye and became known as "Cockeyed." He knew where he was from the sound of the wheels. "When they rattle, I'm on hard ground," he explained. "When they don't rattle, I generally look over the side to see where she's a-going." When Charlie died in 1879, it was discovered that "he" had been christened "Charlotte." Since Charlotte had voted in Santa Cruz, California, elections, neighbors claimed that she had introduced women's suffrage to the West.*

Right: *Hank Monk, "the world's greatest reinsman," drove Horace Greeley from Carson City, Nevada, to Placerville, California—a distance of 109 miles—in ten hours. Greeley, who had to make a speech in Placerville, urged Hank to drive fast, and Hank drove so furiously that Greeley begged him to stop.*

Uncle John Gibbons was the veteran of scores of near disasters on the road. Once, while in an Austin, Nevada, saloon, he was challenged to go down in the North Star Mine, which was reputed to be haunted. He put the matter straight for the barflies.

"I'm afeared of mines, and I don't want to drop down none o' them thar straight holes; but I tell you what I'll do: You trot your ghost out into the big road, and I'll harness him up and drive him tandem all day with Brown Bill and Dick. I ain't afraid of anything with a bit in his mouth."

Cockeyed Charlie Parkhurst caps the roll of drivers. As the coach raced around a mountain trail in a cloud of dust, Charlie told writer J. Ross Browne that he drove the stage by the sound of the wheels.

"When they rattle, I'm on hard ground," he explained. "When they don't rattle, I generally look over the side to see where she's a-going."

Called "Cockeyed" because he wore a patch to cover up an empty eye socket, his mouth and chin stained with tobacco juice, he was cheerful, rarely used profanity, and, though only five feet, seven inches tall, was broad-shouldered and capable of taking his stage over the roughest roads. He shot dead in their tracks the first two bandits to attempt to rob his stage, so even the wildest desperadoes gave his stage a wide berth.

One day in 1860 Charlie retired and opened up an inn by the road between Santa Cruz and Watsonville. Nineteen years later he died, and when his neighbors got Charlie ready for the funeral, they discovered he was really a woman. Born Charlotte Parkhurst in New Hampshire in 1806, Charlie voted in the Santa Cruz elections, and her fellow townspeople claimed that she was the first to bring women's suffrage to the Golden State.

A driver was supposed to have a huge appetite. Uncle Tom Cooper in the Black Hills claimed that he "could eat a stage horse broiled on toast every morning for breakfast."

Stage drivers were also known for their speed. Horace Greeley rode out of Carson City to Placerville with Hank Monk, one of the West's most renowned drivers. He urged Hank to make good time because he had a speech to give in Placerville. Hank obliged by driving so furiously that Greeley cried for him to stop.

TO REMEMBER HANK MONK
THE WORLD'S GREATEST REINSMAN
WHO DROVE HORACE GREELEY FROM
CARSON CITY TO HERE IN 1859,
MAKING THE 109 MILES IN 10 HOURS
DEDICATED BY
E CLAMPUS VITUS APRIL 30, 1938

Above: *The road to Cripple Creek, Colorado, had its mudholes and its unexpected rocks nicely placed to jolt a passenger out of his seat. A stage halted only for a dire emergency or, in this case, because a photographer was handy.*

Left, top: *When the Hundley Stage Line's coaches reached the halfway house on the road to the mining town of Cripple Creek, it was time to change horses and take a rest.*

Left, bottom: *Stagecoaches and freight wagons ate one another's dust along the busy road to Cripple Creek.*

"Keep your seat, Horace," said Hank. "I'll have you there on time."

When Hank mended his clothes he used copper harness rivets instead of buttons to reinforce the seams. This gave Levi Strauss, pioneer overall manufacturer in the West, the idea of making blue denim pants reinforced by copper rivets at the strain points.

Rough and tough as they might be, drivers were also noted for their warm hearts and their kindness to children. In the Black Hills they carried along gum, candy, and firecrackers to give to kids at lonely stations and ranches. In California they actually sang a lullaby when they carried a baby in the stage. It is hard to imagine a gravel-voiced, bearded cuss of a driver singing:

> Hush a by baby on the stage top;
> When the whip cracks your cradle will rock.
> If the wheels fly off, the cradle will fall,
> Down will come baby cradle and all.

Even in song they did not gloss over the perils of the road.

The stagecoach may not run over western trails today, but it is still bigger than life in story and legend all over the world. This is, in good part, Buffalo Bill Cody's doing. No inconsiderable driver himself, Cody introduced a Concord coach into his Wild West show.

In 1883 Cody telegraphed Luke Voorhees, an old Black Hills driver, to find him a coach to use in the show. The Deadwood stage, which Cody himself had once driven, was the veteran of bandit raids and Indian attacks. Voorhees discovered the venerable old stage abandoned on the prairie and sent it to Colville, now Columbus, Nebraska, where Cody was rehearsing his show.

The stage made a spectacular addition to the last dress rehearsal. The mayor and councilmen of Colville got aboard for a ride. When the Pawnee

When a stage stopped at lonely ranch stations such as this one in Wyoming Territory, the driver often handed out candy to the ranch kids. The stage was a tie between frontier towns and families isolated in the wilds.

Buffalo Bill Cody, famed western scout and stagecoach driver, included the equally famed Deadwood stage in his Wild West show. Cody, who started as an extra hand at the age of twelve on Lew Simpson's freight train, rode pony express as a teenager. In 1883 Cody telegraphed Luke Voorhees, an old Black Hills driver, and asked him to find a stagecoach for his Wild West show. Voorhees found the Deadwood stage—a veteran of Indian and bandit attacks—deserted on the prairie. He sent it to Colville, Nebraska (now called Columbus), where Cody was rehearsing his show. The coach was taken along on a tour of the United States and even went with Cody to Europe. Once it sank to the bottom of the Mississippi River in a riverboat wreck above New Orleans. When the coach was rescued from the water, it was found to be in good condition despite the dunking.

Scouts attacked with war whoops and the shooting of cartridge blanks, the half-broken mules pulling the coach bolted and went racing around the track, while the first distinguished guests to ride the Deadwood stage in the show shouted in terror.

The mules had gentled down quite a bit by 1887, the year of Queen Victoria's Jubilee, when Cody brought his Wild West show to London. According to Don Russell in *The Lives and Legends of Buffalo Bill*, he proudly assisted the Prince of Wales and four kings—Leopold II of Belgium, Christian IX of Denmark, George I of Greece, and Albert of Saxony—into the stage. He climbed up on the driver's seat of the sturdy old Concord and cracked his whip, and off they went.

"Colonel, you never held four kings like these before," said the Prince of Wales.

"I've held four kings," replied Cody, "but four kings and the Prince of Wales makes a royal flush, such as no man ever held before."

He'd spoken like a true stagecoach driver. Charlie Parkhurst would have been proud of him.

When the Homestake Mine in Lead, South Dakota, shipped $250,000 in gold bullion on the Deadwood Treasure Wagon, Wells, Fargo & Company guards rode shotgun to insure safe delivery.

Above: *Shaw's Fast Freight Line carried the overland mail and Wells, Fargo & Company's express between Sacramento and San Francisco, California. The departure of the stage always brought out a crowd.*

Below: *In frontier Oklahoma much of the U.S. mail moved in coaches drawn by two span of mules.*

STAGECOACH IN OAK CREEK CANYON by David Miller

COLLECTION OF MR. AND MRS. A. H. TRAUTWEIN

THE SUPPLY WAGON by Jim Reynolds
FRANKLIN MINT GALLERY OF AMERICAN ART

A group of Coloradans have discovered that a stagecoach can be used for purposes other than travel. Mounting an undesirable atop the stage, they prepare to hang him.

Above: *The stage corral of Tallmadge & Lilley at Boulder, Colorado, was the heart of the area's transportation. A stage corral not only housed the horses and coaches, but also provided a nerve center of communications for the townspeople. Drivers and passengers alike relayed the news and gossip that they had picked up along the road.*

Below: *From the studiedly nonchalant boy perched atop a rear wheel as tall as himself to the dignified ladies and gentlemen seated atop the tallyho coach, these pioneer Dakotans are ready to set out on an excursion to Hot Springs in the Black Hills.*

The stagecoach "Maggie" brought holiday-bent Coloradans to Idaho Springs, a pioneer spa, where they put up at the frame Bebee House.

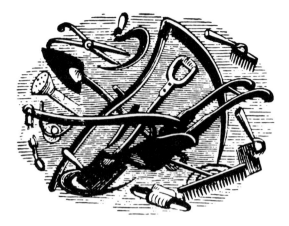

SODBUSTERS & RANCHERS

THE SURREY with the fringe on top celebrated in the musical *Oklahoma* was indeed a popular family vehicle among ranch and farm families of the Old West. Capacious and comfortable with its sweeping fender, leather dash, velvet carpet, cloth upholstery, black body, and Brewster green gear, it gave mother, father, and children a glow of pride when they rode to church on Sunday or went on an outing. It might have been made by Brewster and Company or by Hassett and Hodge, the Amesbury, Massachusetts, firm. Hassett and Hodge's bird's-eye maple bodies were prized because they withstood the trying western climate and road conditions. The surrey used in filming the movie *Oklahoma* is now in the Hazard collection in San Diego.

As sodbusters and ranchers pioneered their holdings, a surrey was far in the future. They might have to be content at first with the worn prairie schooner that had brought them to the West. The wagon that took its place was most likely a simple affair with a square box set flat upon rough wooden axles. When passengers were to be carried, a board could be thrown across the top of the body. William Bridges Adams, the English carriage authority of the nineteenth century, described such a wagon as one of "the rudest four-wheeled vehicles used by civilized peoples. They are called wagons, and consist of an oblong case of rough planks, beneath which the wheels are attached, the fore wheels being contrived to turn or lock very slightly. They are used with one or two horses, whether for farm or other purposes. When they are used for personal conveyance, a simple contrivance is resorted to. To lessen concussion, a kind of frame chair, affixed to two beams of elastic wood, is placed inside for the principal sitters; and if there be others, they rough it out as they best can."

These wagons were made by local wagonmakers. Mathew Lyons, the first wagonmaker in the state of Oregon, set up his shop on the banks of Elk Creek at Yoncalla. Blacksmith Charles Applegate made the irons for the wagons, out of boiler plate that came from the nearby Hudson's Bay Company post.

Crude as these wagons may have been, they were sophisticated compared to the wagons built by Norwegian emigrants. Norwegian homesteaders ascended the tributary rivers of the Mississippi and Missouri as far as they could go. With axe and saw they hewed four solid wheels out of the trunk of a tree growing on the riverbank. They fashioned two long planks and laid them across timber axles. This massive *kubberulle,* as they called it, could haul crops to market and grain to the mill, and could take the homesteaders to quilting and husking bees. It carried a settler on his last journey to the church graveyard at the same creaking speed with which it performed less mournful tasks. Only a few *kubberulles* have survived. Vesterheim, the Norwegian-American museum in Decorah, Iowa, has a sturdy example that could still haul Norse parents and their shock-haired kids to church.

As settlements spread, far and away the most suitable all-purpose family wagon among both ranchers and sodbusters was the buckboard. It had no trouble with breaking a spring, because it did not have any. The original vehicle had a seat mounted on a single board bolted to the front and rear axles. The elasticity of the board reduced the shocks as the wagon bucked over the rough roads. Later on a slatted frame replaced the board, but the vehicle still counted on the give-and-take of pliable wood to soften the ride. Anywhere from Texas to the Dakotas it was the ideal wagon to drive into town to drop off produce or eggs, and pick up a load of supplies. A rumble seat was installed on some so that the kids could ride along, but it could be taken off when more cargo space was needed. In the ranch country even the mailman drove a buckboard, and to a cowboy the very expression "buckboard driver" came to mean the mail carrier.

The buckboard may have been the most popular vehicle back at the ranch, but out on the range the chuck wagon was the center of life itself. Immediately after the Civil War the first kitchen wagons on the Texas range were called commissaries. Before 1866 they were often two-wheeled carts pulled by a yoke of oxen. In the spring of that year Charles Goodnight, the rancher whose name is kept alive by the fame of the Goodnight trails, bought

the gear of an army wagon. It had iron axles instead of wood. He hired a Parker County woodworker to rebuild the wagon box of seasoned bois d'arc and placed a chuck box at the rear end. Six oxen pulled the first chuck wagon.

Later on a chuck wagon was usually pulled by four horses or mules. It had wide tires for traction in rough country. It had a standard bed, but extra sideboards gave it additional room to carry the cowboys' bedrolls and personal gear. Canvas wagon sheets were stretched over arched bows and tied against the sun and the rain.

"Our first mess boxes were goods boxes," remembered veteran cowboy Mark Withers in a manuscript quoted by Wayne Gard in *The Chisholm Trail*. "We put bacon, coffee, and flour in a box in the middle of the wagon. We had hides stretched under the wagon and put utensils there. We also had a water barrel with the spout out in front of the wagon. Later we turned it so the spout was out on one side. I liked the barrel spout out in front better because it didn't get broken as often."

A cowboy might call the chuck wagon "the crumb castle," but he valued its presence in the outfit as much as he valued the cook. "Cookie" drew higher pay than a cowpuncher, and his authority was second only to that of the trail boss.

"Crossin' a cook is as risky as braidin' a mule's

Left: *The Dry Cimarron Ranch in New Mexico was the home ranch of the Scottish-owned Prairie Cattle Company, Ltd. About 1888 the wagon boss, Robert Haley, posed on horseback in the center of his men.*

Below: *Abilene, Kansas, at the end of the Chisholm Trail, is where cattle driven from Texas were loaded aboard Union Pacific trains for shipment to the stockyards in Chicago.*

tail," was a range saying that had more than a trifle of wisdom in it.

"Cookie" drove the chuck wagon, and he kept it and its harness in shape. He was in charge of the cowboys' belongings, held stakes during a bet, doctored and pulled teeth, barbered a fellow's hair on the night before the outfit reached town, and sewed on buttons.

Each cook had his own ideas about how his chuck box should be arranged, and the nosy individual who tampered with it was asking for trouble. Invariably, following Goodnight's example, it was built into the back end. It was a closed upright cupboard with partitions, shelves, and drawers for food and utensils.

"Its rear end sloped outward from top to bottom," says Gard, "like the front of an antique writing desk. The piece across the sloping end was hinged at the bottom so that the cook could lower it to a horizontal position. This allowed it to serve as a kitchen table in front of the cabinet. The cabinet door was held in this position by ropes or chains or, more often, by a prop resting on the ground."

A cowboy's "eatin' irons"; a five-gallon keg or jar of sourdough, upon which the cook's reputation depended; a sack of flour; cans of coffee, almost always Arbuckle's; salt; condiments; and such staples as beans, salt pork, dried fruits, canned tomatoes, onions, potatoes, sugar, molasses, pepper, and lard were, as noted by Gard, all in the chuck box. Out

Above: *At mealtime cowboys of the L I T Ranch in the Texas Panhandle gathered around the chuck wagon. The cowboys were on a roundup in the 1880s. The chuck wagon was the center of a cowboy's open-air home. "In the shade of the wagon" was cowboy talk for taking life easy.*

Left: *Bill Jones, cook, prepares a hearty meal while hungry cowpunchers share yarns on a roundup on Yellow Creek in northwestern Colorado.*

of these fixings and what he could scrounge up along the trail, a cook produced suppers of beans, known as "Pecos strawberries"; son-of-a-bitch stew, said to have everything in it but the horns, hide, and hoofs of a slaughtered steer; sourdough biscuits, not so lovingly called belly cheaters by those who ate them; and six-shooter coffee, boiled, it was said, so long that a six-shooter could float on its surface.

There was a drawer for horse liniment for aches and pains; powdered alum good for rope burns, boils, and sores; coal oil; turpentine; Epsom salts; mutton tallow and camphor spirits; and a bottle of whiskey in case of snakebites. (Cowboys were expected to be stone sober on the trail.) A smaller box for heavy skillets, pots, and Dutch ovens sat beneath the chuck

box or in front of it. Bedrolls and personal equipment were also placed in front of the chuck box. On the side opposite the water barrel was a toolbox containing branding irons, equipment to shoe a horse, axes, and shovels. The wagon also carried grain for the animals that pulled it.

Beneath the wagon was the possum belly, or the caboose. In the Southwest it was known as the cooney or the *cuna,* which is Spanish for "cradle." This was a green cowhide stretched to the running gear of the wagon. The head and forelegs were lashed to the front, and the hind legs were tied to the rear axle. The sides were tied to the sides of the bed. The rear of the possum belly was tied more loosely, and it was filled with rocks while drying so

Above: *The cook has built his fire a few feet from the chuck wagon on the range in Las Animas County, Colorado. The fire meant light and warmth to a cowboy. A stern law of the camp demanded that a cowboy must not ride his horse so close to the fire that he would raise a cloud of dust while a meal was being prepared or eaten.*

Right: *The chuck wagon went first when the cowboys were on the trail. Thus it was able to keep ahead of the dust kicked up by the cattle. It stopped at the nooning place to serve a cold lunch from the flap board and then hurried on down the trail to the spot picked for the night's camp.*

that it would hang down lower at the rear of the wagon. This made it easier for "Cookie" or a cowpuncher to drop fuel wood, buffalo chips, or cow chips into the possum belly.

Sometimes calves born on the trail could not keep up with their mothers. If a rider saw that a calf was in trouble, he popped it into the possum belly for a bouncing ride. In two or three days it could rejoin its mother. At night a small cowboy might slip into the possum belly to sleep out of the rain and to keep warm.

On the trail the chuck wagon went first, far ahead of the dust kicked up by the plodding herd of cattle. It would stop at the nooning place to serve up a cold lunch from the flap board, then rattle on down the trail to the spot selected for the next camp. Once the chuck wagon was set up, it became the center of a cowboy's open-air home. Its sheets could be spread out and supported by poles to make a shady pavilion against the torrid sun. "In the shade of the wagon" understandably became cowboy talk for taking life easy.

A cooking fire was built a few feet from the wagon. The cook used chips from the possum belly, or "prairie coal," and wood. In wet weather he might pour gunpowder into his pistol, wad it loosely, and kindle a blaze by firing the gun with its muzzle close to a scrap of cloth. The fire was also light and warmth, and cowboys who were off duty sat around the wagon and told stories and jokes, played practical jokes on one another, and wrestled. Sometimes they sang the songs that have captured the imaginations of people all over the world who have never seen a chuck wagon. There was stern etiquette in at least one respect. A cowboy was not allowed to ride his horse so near that he raised a cloud of dust over the wagon when a meal was being prepared or eaten.

The bedrolls were taken out of the wagon and spread out for the night. A man went to what he called his Tucson bed, "made by lying on your stomach and covering that with your back." Sometimes the trail boss would aim the tongue of the wagon at the North Star before he turned in, so that the outfit would know which way to get started in the morning.

If an outfit was big enough, the chuck wagon was given assistance by a trailer bouncing along behind, which was affectionately known as the pie wagon. There might also be a two-wheeled cart called the chip wagon; a "hoodlum wagon" that carried the water barrel, wood, and branding irons; a "blattin' cart" into which newborn calves were loaded on the trail; and a bed wagon into which bedding and other gear might be loaded. The bed wagon also could serve as an ambulance for the sick or injured. Last of all, somewhere in the neighborhood there might be a strictly unauthorized vehicle known as a cat wagon. In it women of uncertain virtue and nomadic instincts plied their ancient trade.

Some vehicles used on the ranch were unsuitable for trail drives. The "doll baby" was a two-wheeled cart used for hauling small loads around the outbuildings. A hay wagon had racks instead of a wagon box, so that the grass dried as it was being transported. A fence wagon carried tools and materials to build or repair fences. A couple of cowboys might drive a trouble wagon loaded with tools and

spare parts on a fix-it round of windmills, pumps, and water troughs. A trouble wagon also carried salt to the range for the cattle to lick.

At Harold Warp's Pioneer Village in Minden, Nebraska, a cowboy's chuck wagon from Texas rests next to a sheepherder's wagon, a situation that, given the animosity between cattlemen and sheepmen, would scarcely have happened on the range. Whether a cowboy or a sheepherder would ever admit it or not, the sheep wagon had much in common with the chuck wagon. It too was rugged and capacious, and was home to hardy men living in the outdoors. It usually contained a stove and bunk, and possibly a table and benches. It carried food for the men and grain for the horses, and had a place for the sheep dog to curl up and sleep. Often a big sheep outfit was accompanied by a cook wagon, a supply wagon, and a buckboard for running errands.

The last few decades of the American western frontier were also the years of America's greatest production of horse-drawn vehicles. An Indianapolis company was making 200,000 road carts a year. In 1860 there were sixty carriage makers in New Haven, Connecticut, alone, and G. and D. Cook and Company, which produced a complete carriage every hour, could claim to be the largest carriage maker in the world. Studebaker in South Bend, Indiana, made a wagon every five minutes.

Across the West wagons proliferated. There were the durable Studebaker farm wagons with their green bodies, red trim, and red wheels. There were the grain wagons with their floors tightly crafted so as not to lose a precious kernel, Democrat wagons—special spring wagons used on ranches because of their light weight—and ordinary spring wagons, often called the poor man's surrey because a man could place a backseat in the cargo space to give his family a ride. There were oil wagons dispensing the kerosene refined in the East by "Coal Oil Johnny" Rockefeller, peddlers' wagons, called hand wagons in the ranch country, and show wagons. The show wagon of J. H. Bowman the Showman, for whom Fred Astaire danced when he was a small boy, is on display at Pioneer Village in Minden.

Above: *A sodbuster's log cabin-dugout near Osborne, Kansas, was anything but a thing of beauty, but it provided shelter against the heat of summer and the cold of winter.*

Left: *These buffalo hunters of the 1860s are drying hides by spreading them out beneath the Texas sun. Hunters decimated the bison herds, and cattle took over the range in their stead.*

Below: *Farmers carried their produce to market in wagons. A grain wagon had tightly fitted floors so as not to lose a single kernel of wheat.*

Studebaker even made a patent sprinkler wagon to wet down dusty roads. Plattsmouth, Nebraska, as befits one of the state's oldest cities, exhibits a pioneer Studebaker Celebrated Patent Sprinkler, which served as a street cleaner in its later life until the late 1920s, when it was taken to the cemetery and used as a water-storage tank. People took water from it to water graves. The mayor, a shop superintendent of the Birmingham Refrigerator Express, and the chief mechanic in the railroad shops fixed up the wagon; it is now in a park on Main Street.

A calaboose wagon took outlaws to jail. A hearse took the dead to their graves. With its gleaming silver, plate-glass windows, and black drapery and tassels, the hearse was designed to give deceased citizens a last ride in luxury. It was all very impressive, but this did not keep cowboys from giving the hearse one of their down-to-earth names. To a cowboy a hearse was "a cold meat wagon."

As pioneers prospered, buggies began to appear in the West. Cowboys scoffed at the ranch owner who rode about his domain in a buggy, and called

Left, top: *Beginning in 1877, wagon trains carried produce and wool from ranches to the Belen, New Mexico, warehouse of the Becker family. After being loaded with supplies for the ranches, the wagons headed back home.*

Left, bottom: *On the huge Dalrymple Farm in Minnesota in 1878, sodbusting was a vast undertaking that involved platoons of machines and wagons. Plowing, harrowing, and seeding were done on a scale made possible by the flatness of the plains and by the wheeled machines, which in a few decades were to bring the frontier to an end.*

Below: *Towns sprang up on the sodbuster frontier, and farm wagons mixed with town wagons on the still unpaved streets.*

him a "buggy boss," because they suspected that he did not know how to sit his horse any too well.

Americans invented the buggy. Its frame was based on a German wagon model, but it had a light body borrowed from a small English carriage. Its four small wheels were made of well-seasoned hickory. Elliptical springs mounted at right angles to the traveling direction gave it an easy ride.

When his family grew too big for a buggy, a farmer or rancher who had the means usually bought a carriage. A quality carriage, such as those made by G. and D. Cook, had case-hardened iron axles and English tempered-steel springs. It was roomy, with a well-trimmed interior and cushioned seats. Visitors from the East were astounded to encounter such handsome rigs on the streets of Cheyenne, San Antonio, and other western towns.

The Oklahoma Land Rush saw an amazing turnout of frontier vehicles. Gigs, buckboards, carts, prairie schooners, farm wagons, carriages, and even two bicycles lined up as 100,000 people prepared to pour into the Oklahoma District. At noon on April 22, 1889, a rifle cracked as a signal. Eyewitness Seth Humphrey, a young Minnesotan, described the historic event in his journal:

"The line broke with a huge, crackling roar. The one thundering moment of horseflesh by the mile quivering in its first leap forward was a gift of the gods, and its like will never come again. The next instant we were in a crush of vehicles whizzing past us like a calamity."

Humphrey and a friend rode the two bikes in the great rush for land. He noted with satisfaction that "at least we two of the bicycle corps did not have to mix up with the jam of horses about the place." He was not quite so pleased when his tires were punctured by the sharp stubble and ruts left by the avalanche of vehicles. It rather spoiled being in on the last great forward movement of the frontier, carried out by the most incredible and varied array of horse-drawn vehicles that the world has seen gathered in one place.

Above: *On a bright day in 1886 the Surene Pike family of Jefferson, Custer County, Nebraska, turned out in their Sunday best. Complete with buggies, horses, and croquet set, they posed for photographer Solomon D. Butcher. Pioneer families could send such pictures to relatives and friends back east as proof that they were civilizing the frontier.*

Left: *A South Dakota farm couple put on their best clothes to ride into town in their buggy to shop for necessities or, on Sundays, to go to church.*

Below: *When a North Dakota pioneer family moved, they loaded their belongings onto farm wagons and set out for their new homestead.*

Above: *The lumbering frontier also rolled west on wheels. Huge log wagons carried logs out of the forest. This wagon is exhibited at the Institute of Texan Cultures in San Antonio.*

Below: *Years after the sodbuster frontier had faded into history, pioneers of Barber County, Kansas, and their descendants gathered with the old wagons to relive the adventurous but difficult times. They might have driven to the reunion in automobiles, but once they had parked the cars on the hill and descended to their wagons, it seemed as though the past and the present were one and the same—especially to the older generation.*

THE COMING OF THE RAILROADS

DANDY TOM FLETCHER, who drove the stage-coach between Topeka and Fort Riley, Kansas, was enjoying a cigar in the lobby of a Topeka hotel. Clad in broadcloth, a turquoise and silver pin in his silk cravat, his hat and gloves by his side, he listened with an amused smile as Cyrus K. Holliday and Edmund G. Ross talked about building the Santa Fe Railway through Kansas. In *Santa Fe* James Marshall tells of their conversation:

"How would you like to drive a steam engine across the plains, Mr. Fletcher?" asked Holliday.

Fletcher indulged in a polite chuckle.

"Reckon it'd be too dirty a job for me, Colonel. Give me my six bays any time."

Across the West the knights of the rein—the mule skinners and bullwhackers and all the other thousands of men who kept commerce rolling down the trails and roads—believed that railroads would never prove practical. Besides, who would want to give up the prestige and challenge of driving a team of matched bays to sit at the throttle of a smoke-belching machine?

For decades there had been talk about a railroad spanning the continent from the Atlantic to the Pacific. As early as 1819 Robert Mills of Baltimore had proposed a rail line from the headwaters of inland navigation to the sunset end of the continent. Explorers and mountain men had reported the feasibility of building a railroad through the Rockies, but nothing seemed likely to come of it. As late as 1848 the *New York Herald* commented on a pro-

jected transcontinental railroad: "This whole project is ridiculous and absurd. Centuries hence it will be time enough to talk of such a railroad."

Dandy Tom and all his friends could hardly be expected to take western railroads seriously, even though railroads were already inching their way along the West Coast. The first railroad in California, twenty-one miles long, linked Sacramento and Folsom in 1856. Wood-burning locomotives pulled a few cars in competition with the stagecoaches. Vaqueros raced the trains of another railroad operating between Los Angeles and Wilmington. They waved in triumph and shouted in Spanish as they sped past the poking black and gold locomotive, which had been shipped around the Horn from the East. The locomotive did not seem to be much more effective than the horse-drawn coach on wooden rails that it had replaced, and the horse-pulled coach had been called the "get out and push" railroad, since this proved necessary whenever the horse balked. In the early 1870s Dr. Dorsey Baker built a thirty-two-mile line from Wallula, Washington, to Walla Walla. He put in wooden rails topped with rawhide, only to have packs of wolves devour the rawhide off the tracks. He next used scrap iron, which reared up in death-dealing snakeheads through the wooden floors of his coaches. The doctor bought only the wheels for his coaches and built his own rolling stock.

The Union Pacific Railroad was the child of the Pacific Railroad Act of 1862, which was passed by Congress after a number of preliminary surveys

Above: *Construction on the Union Pacific Railroad began in Nebraska in 1865. Locomotives were dragged across the ice of the unbridged Missouri River and placed upon the first few miles of track. Wagonloads of ties were hauled across the prairies. The workmen put down the ties and rails across the unbroken plains, progressing at the rate of 1.5 miles a day, and by 1867 they had extended the line west of Fort Kearney.*

Below: *In 1872 the Santa Fe Railway's tracks came to an end near Hutchinson, Kansas. The founder of the town, C. C. Hutchinson, took this photo.*

had been made of possible routes across the continent. The central route taken by fur traders and trappers, emigrants, and the Overland Stage had finally been selected. Supervised by Maj. Gen. Grenville Dodge, crews of Irish immigrants and other workers would drive the Union Pacific Railroad west, and Samuel Skerry Montague and his Chinese would drive the Central Pacific's tracks east across the High Sierras.

Construction on the Union Pacific, which started out from Omaha, Nebraska, did not begin until 1865, but the Central Pacific broke ground in 1863 at what is now the intersection of Front and K streets in Sacramento, and began to build up through the Mother Lode country towards the Sierra crest. Rails, horses, scrapers, hand shovels, pickaxes, and black powder to blast a way through mountain shoulders were shipped around Cape Horn. When the Union Pacific began construction, locomotives were dragged across the frozen ice of the as yet unbridged Missouri River and placed upon the few miles of tracks that had been laid. Wagonloads of ties were hauled across the prairies after Thomas C. Durant announced for the railroad, "I need a million cross ties—and right now! And ten thousand rails and a few other things, for a beginning."

Graders worked at least 100 miles ahead of track crews. Rails were rolled to crews on small, light horse-drawn cars that operated on the rails.

When a car was empty, it was tipped off the tracks. The horse pulled it back to where it could be placed on the tracks again and reloaded. The rails advanced across the plains at the astounding rate of 1.5 miles a day. One day the tracklayers put down 2 miles of track. A swarm of wagons was employed by both the eastern and western crews. Jerk-line teams of fourteen mules or oxen pulled huge freight wagons loaded with construction materials or supplies for the railroad construction gangs.

A whole mobile town kept pace with railhead across Nebraska and Wyoming. Barracks, gambling halls, drinking tents, and false-front stores moved by rail flatcar and wagon as construction forged ahead. A 40-by-100-foot big top that housed a bar, a brass band, and a dance floor advanced with the rails, since it was considered an integral part of "Hell on Wheels," as the nomadic town was called by the Irish workmen.

In the West the Chinese cut tunnels through the mountains and built sheds to ward off the heavy snows that threatened to stop the line in the winter. They came down out of the mountains at last and worked eastward over the Nevada and Utah deserts. Finally, on May 10, 1869, at Promontory, Utah, the rails were ready to meet. Only a fifty-foot gap separated the Irishmen and the Chinese, the East and the West. Dignitaries came from New York, Boston, Chicago, and San Francisco. The Central Pacific's

HARPER'S WEEKLY. [SEPTEMBER 7, 1867.

CHICAGO HISTORICAL SOCIETY

On August 6, 1867, Chief Turkey Foot and a war party of Cheyenne Indians attacked a working crew on the Union Pacific Railroad in Nebraska.

"Jupiter" rolled to the end of the tracks, and the Union Pacific's "Number 119" rolled up to the opposite side of the gap. Bret Harte immortalized the historic moment in a poem that captured the world's imagination:

> What was it the engines said,
> Pilots touching, head to head
> Facing on a single track,
> Half a world behind each back?

The gap was closed, and a last laurel crosstie from California, magnificently polished and bearing a silver plate, was put in place. There was a silver spike from Nevada's Comstock Lode, a spike of iron, gold, and silver alloy from Arizona Territory, and silver spikes from Idaho and Montana. When these were driven in, only one spike was needed—a gold spike made by a San Francisco jewelry firm.

Leland Stanford, president of the Central Pacific and former governor of California, stepped forward and grasped a silver-headed maul. He swung and missed. Teamster Alexander Toponce was present, and he wrote down what happened:

Left, top: By late 1867 the Union Pacific tracks had reached Archer, Wyoming. From that point on, white-topped wagons were ready to roll farther west, bearing supplies for the tracklayers.

Left, bottom: A wheel scraper outfit moved the dirt during the construction of the right-of-way for the Eastern Oklahoma Railway.

Below: Chief engineer Samuel Skerry Montague of the Central Pacific (on the left) and Maj. Gen. Grenville Dodge, chief engineer of the Union Pacific, shake hands as the Central Pacific's "Jupiter" and the Union Pacific's "No. 119" meet face to face at Promontory, Utah, on May 10, 1869. Men from the East and from the West wave champagne bottles in anticipation of a toast. The dream of a transcontinental railroad has been realized.

Above: *A bell-stacked locomotive and pioneer passenger cars cross the Canyon Diablo Bridge in Arizona. This bridge was one of the Santa Fe Railway's early engineering masterpieces.*

Right, top: *The stage to Cripple Creek, Colorado, picked up passengers from a train as stage lines became feeders for the railroads that were penetrating the once remote areas of the West.*

Right, bottom: *An early Santa Fe train pulls into the Burlingame, Kansas, depot, where a horse-drawn bus waits to take passengers to their destinations.*

"What a howl went up! Irish, Chinese, Mexicans and everybody yelled with delight. 'He missed it. Yee!' The engineers blew the whistles and rang their bells.

"Then Stanford tried it again and tapped the spike, and the telegraph operators had fixed their instruments so that the tap was reported in all the offices east and west, and set bells to tapping in hundreds of towns and cities."

Spectators carried away splinters of the last ties as souvenirs. In the East President Grant made the official announcement that the Atlantic and Pacific were linked by rail. In Philadelphia the Liberty Bell rang out the good news, 100-gun salutes were fired in New York's Castle Garden, and *Te Deums* were sung in churches across the land. In almost every city and town the night closed with fireworks and speeches that would have done justice to the Fourth of July.

Almost a century after the event President John F. Kennedy summed up its significance:

"We need not read deeply into the history of the United States to become aware of the great and vital role which the railroads have played in the opening up and developing of this great nation. As our frontier moved westward, it was the railroads that bore the great tide of Americans to areas of new opportunities and new hope."

President Kennedy was essentially right, although as late as 1895 emigrant wagons were still rolling through South Pass on their way over the Oregon Trail. Not everybody could afford the price of rail transportation. For at least forty years the age of the stagecoach, the emigrant wagon, and the freight wagon overlapped with the age of the railroad in the West.

For the most part the old day felt no rivalry with the new. Westerners knew firsthand the truth

Above: *A wagonload of Wells, Fargo & Company express and a representative selection of station idlers wait for the train at Guthrie, Oklahoma.*

Right: *Herds of buffalo cross the tracks while the tall-stacked locomotive waits, panting, for them to pass.*

Below: *In September, 1889, the Santa Fe Railway distributed seed wheat in Guthrie for the first winter wheat crop. The sodbusters gave their notes for the seed and paid them the following year, when the crop was harvested.*

in the old saying that "western travel is rough on women and oxen." They realized the vast savings in freight costs. In 1865 it cost $27 to haul 100 pounds of freight 1,200 miles from Fort Leavenworth to Salt Lake City. A cargo that cost $40,000 to transport by wagon could be hauled by the railroad twenty years later for $1,500.

It is true that cowboys around Dodge City, Kansas, delighted in shooting out the headlights of locomotives at night. The Indians, who had at first raided the tracklaying crews, now contented themselves in the main with lassoing the poles that bore the railroad telegraph, tearing down the wires, and riding off into the hills to hide them. They built fires at pole bases and watched the poles burn with patient care. Repair crews had to dash out and restore service on the singing wires.

The buffalo proved to be more of a problem. They wandered about on the tracks and blocked trains. Engines were equipped with water-squirting devices to frighten the animals out of the way. There were also other difficulties. Mormon crickets sometimes hopped about on the tracks in such dense concentrations that the drive wheels of a locomotive spun helplessly over their crushed bodies. Flights of grasshoppers piled up two inches deep on the tracks near Colorado Springs in 1873 and stopped the trains.

As the rails pushed farther into the high mountain country, winter snows proved to be almost insurmountable. The snow in the Rockies was piled so high during one winter that a locomotive pulling two cars was derailed six times between Ironton and Silverton on the Silverton Railroad.

Everyone aboard had to help shovel away the snow and pry the cars back on the tracks.

Sometimes there was high comedy as new lines reached once isolated towns. When the Southern Pacific entered Tucson in 1880 and tied it to San Francisco, the mayor of Tucson wrote a telegram to the Pope:

"To His Holiness, the Pope of Rome, Italy. The mayor of Tucson begs the honor of reminding Your Holiness that this ancient and honorable pueblo was founded by the Spaniards under the sanction of the Church more than three centuries ago, and to inform Your Holiness that a railroad from San Francisco, California, now connects us with the Christian world. R. N. Leatherwood, mayor. Asking your benediction...."

Three Tucsonians persuaded the operator not to send the wire. They concocted a reply that "arrived" that evening:

"His Holiness the Pope acknowledges with appreciation receipt of your telegram informing him that the ancient city of Tucson at last has been connected by rail with the outside world and sends his benediction, but for his own satisfaction would ask, where in hell is Tucson?"

As the rails spread out from the first trunk lines,

Right, top: *Railroads were eager to advertise their services in the late nineteenth century. The ad on the left, done in the 1890s, claims that trains are much safer and more comfortable than the hurtling stagecoaches. The ad on the right is aimed at the railroads themselves. It urges them to purchase the "Sheffield Velocipede Hand-Car," which became the preferred way for many track crews to check out the track. It was operated by a rowing movement and would not jump the track even at speeds of twenty miles per hour.*

Right, bottom: *The concept of using the wind to propel a vehicle was adapted to the rails. In this illustration a sailing car on the Kansas Pacific Railroad frightens a pair of horses grazing in a nearby field. Sailing cars sped track crews to scenes of trouble.*

Below: *The Santa Fe operated mule-drawn ambulances to take injured railroad workers to the company hospital.*

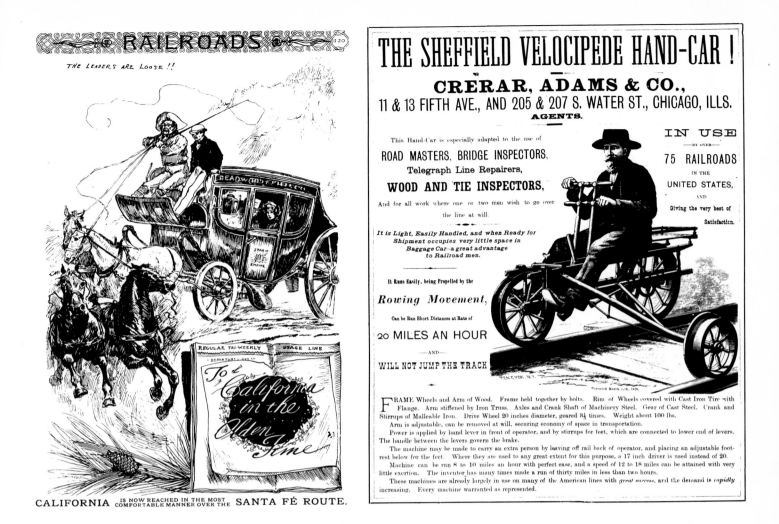

THE LEADERS ARE LOOSE !!

the freight and stagecoach lines stopped running. When the Denver & Rio Grande reached Trinidad, Colorado, the last Barlow & Sanderson coach pulled out on the morning of May 3, 1876. The last Barlow & Sanderson stage into Santa Fe operated on January 24, 1880. The last stage from Bozeman to Helena, Montana, left on June 20, 1883. The coach, pulled by a six-horse team, was decorated with red, white, and blue bunting. On February 19, 1887, a crowd gathered in front of Cheyenne's Inter-Ocean Hotel to watch the last Black Hills stage pull out. It was the "Wyoming," and John Nunan, the oldest driver on the line, was to handle the ribbons. Nunan got so drunk that he couldn't do the job. Hardly anybody blamed him, because, while almost everybody welcomed the railroad, people realized that a colorful period in the West was drawing to an end.

The teamsters had always sung songs, but now they added a new verse:

Now all you jolly wagoners, who have got good wives,
Go home to your farms and there spend your lives.
When your corn is all cribbed and your small grain is sowed,
You'll have nothing to do but curse the railroad.

When the Santa Fe Railway reached Raton Pass on the Santa Fe Trail, the line had to deal with

Above: *A tallyho coach takes excursionists to the rim of the Grand Canyon from the nearest Santa Fe station.*

Left, top: *Uncle Dick Wootton, mountain man and freighter, built a pioneer toll road for wagons through Raton Pass, Colorado. When the Santa Fe Railway sent emissaries to buy the road as a railroad right-of-way, he thought hard but finally agreed to sell. "Well, I guess I'll have to get out of the way of the locomotive," he said.*

Left, bottom: *Uncle Dick lived in this homestead near Raton Pass until it was destroyed by fire in 1891.*

Below: *Mechanized wheels running on tracks operate on three levels at a Black Hills, South Dakota, mine. The horse-drawn wagon in the lower right-hand corner is being used for transportation to the roughest areas and for making deliveries from the tracks.*

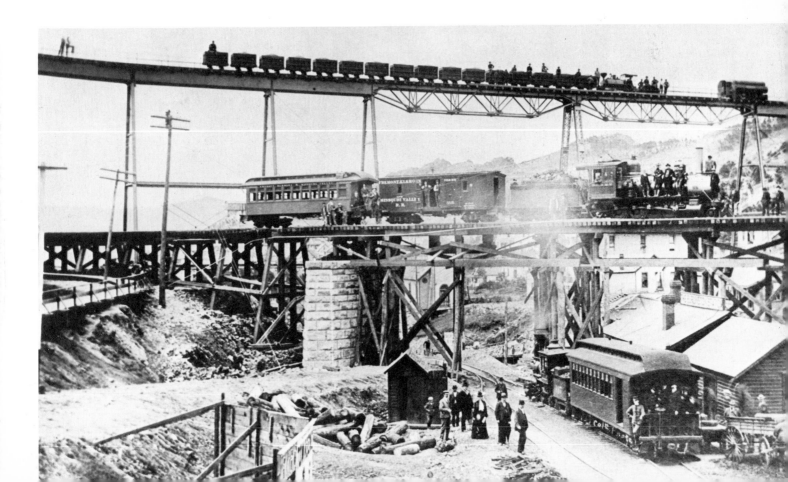

Sometimes I sit here half dreaming, after the fashion of old men, and almost expecting to hear the crack of the stage driver's whip and the rattle of the stage wheels, when the whistle of a locomotive as it comes tearing down the mountain reminds me that the old days are gone, and we have a new order of things. Then, when I look around for the old fellows who handled the reins over six or eight horses and kept a lookout for Indians at the same time, and my old partners in the freighting business I don't find any of them, and that impresses upon me the fact that what I am telling about now happened a long time ago.

The time was indeed long ago, but there is still a green memory in America for the distant crack of whips and the shout of command, for Wheels West.

Above: *The first Santa Fe Railway train rolled into Albuquerque, New Mexico, on April 22, 1880.*

Left, top: *In this wood engraving, done in 1869, a Great Plains station of the Union Pacific is presented as a colorful place where dudes from the East rub elbows with the rough citizens of the West.*

Left, bottom: *A tangle of buggies—the taxicabs of yesteryear—awaits the train at the Santa Fe depot at Topeka, Kansas, in 1880.*

Above: *Wagon and auto coexist in Trinidad, Colorado, as horse-drawn hearses move down the street in solemn procession, past some of the first automobiles introduced into the West. The hearses carried the bodies of coal miners massacred at nearby Ludlow during the strike of 1913–1914.*

Right, top: *A man demonstrates a jack on the Star Bakery delivery wagon in San Bernardino, California, as the delivery boy gravely looks on. In western towns horse-drawn wagons continued to be used well into the twentieth century.*

Right, bottom: *Ezra Meeker followed the Oregon Trail over the plains and the mountains with an emigrant wagon train in 1852. In 1906, at the age of seventy-six, he fashioned a covered wagon out of three surviving pioneer wagons. Hitching a pair of oxen to the wagon, he retraced the Oregon Trail to Independence, Missouri, and then rolled on through the nation all the way to New York City, where police officers stopped him for breaking a law against driving cattle on the streets. "All right, boys," said Meeker. "You take the cattle." The police were nonplussed. When the mayor heard about it, he gave the doughty old pioneer the keys to the city. Later Meeker drove over the Oregon Trail in an automobile and stopped at Fort Bridger, Wyoming, where he was photographed standing before the ruins of Jim Bridger's once bustling post. In 1923 he flew over the route of the Oregon Trail in an airplane. Buttonholed by reporters on a trip to Washington, D.C., Meeker expressed nostalgia for the old-fashioned way of traveling: "If you want to get the feel of what it took to pioneer America, you can't just whiz over it. You'll have to do some walking along interesting stretches of old trails, and around the storied landmarks. I footed it every step of the way from Iowa to Oregon in 1852. My wife and our baby boy rode in the covered wagon. Didn't hurt me to hoof it."*

Bibliography

MANUSCRIPTS, LETTERS, PAMPHLETS, and DOCUMENTS

Amesbury, Robert. *Nobles' Emigrant Trail*. Susanville, Calif., 1967.

Arnold, Elwyn. Letter of May 24, 1971.

Guthrie, A. B., Jr. "Treasure State." *Montana,* Centennial Edition. Butte, Mont., 1964.

Hieb, David L. *Fort Laramie*. National Park Service, Washington, D.C., 1954.

Historical Album of Colorado. Rush to the Rockies Centennial Commission, Denver, 1959.

Holt, Mamie Belle. *A Tavern Houses History*. Washington, Ark., 1965.

"In These Golden Tracks." Idaho Historical Society, Boise, Idaho, 1959.

Isaacs, L. W., Director of Publication. *Wyoming*. Wyoming 75th Anniversary Commission, Douglas, Wyo., 1965.

Jones, John W. "1858–59 Journal of John W. Jones." Everett Graff Collection, Newberry Library, Chicago.

Kruse, Anne Applegate. *Yoncalla Home of the Eagles*. Drain, Ore., 1950.

Main, J. R. K. "Early Transportation in Canada." Department of Transport, Ottawa, Canada, n.d.

Meacham, Walter. "Applegate Trail." Oregon Council, American Pioneer Trails Association, Salem, Ore., 1947.

National Golden Spike Centennial Celebration. Golden Spike Centennial Commission, Ogden, Utah, 1969.

Nichols, Claude W., Jr. "The South Road: Its Development and Significance." A thesis presented to the Department of History and the Graduate School of the University of Oregon, June 1953.

Overholser, Joel F. *Centenary History of Fort Benton, Montana*. Fort Benton Centennial Association, Fort Benton, Mont., 1946.

——. *A Souvenir History of Fort Benton, Montana*. Fort Benton, Mont., n.d.

Randall, Benjamin. "Across the United States—1862." Manuscript in collection of R. S. Weeks, Glen Ellyn, Ill.

Salmon, Cutler. Letter from French Camp, Calif., October 30, 1853. Collection of Elwyn Arnold.

"The Santa Fe Trail: National Survey of Historic Sites and Buildings." National Park Service, Washington, D.C., 1963.

Sargent, Shirley. *Wawona's Yesterdays*. Yosemite Natural History Association, Yosemite National Park, Calif., n.d.

Schuffler, R. Henderson. "Old Ten-Ox Crossing." Texana Program, University of Texas, n.d.

Schultz, Clarence H. "Murphy Wagon Model." Trapper's and Trader's Frontier, Unit VI, Exhibit No. 17. Exhibit Research Report, Jefferson National Expansion Memorial, Saint Louis, December 1964.

Smith, H. Merle. "At the End of the Oregon Trail." An address delivered December 4, 1951, in Portland, Ore. Reprinted by Oregon Savings and Loan League.

"South Boise Wagon Road." Reference Series, No. 94. Idaho Historical Society, Boise, Idaho, n.d.

Utley, Robert M. *Fort Davis*. National Park Service Historical Handbook Series, No. 38. Washington, D.C., 1965.

——. *Fort Union*. National Park Service Historical Handbook Series, No. 35. Washington, D.C., 1962.

Virden, Bill. *The Concord Stage*. San Diego Historical Society, n.d.

Whittenburg, Clarice. *Wyoming*. Cheyenne, Wyo., n.d.

Wiklund, Adeline. "Winter of Death." *These to Remember,* Idaho Poets and Writers Guild, 1962.

Wilkinson, Norman B. "The Conestoga Wagon." Historic Pennsylvania Leaflet No. 5. Historical and Museum Commission, Harrisburg, 1962.

PERIODICALS

Applegate, Jesse. "A Day with the Cow Column in 1843." *Oregon Historical Society Quarterly* 1, No. 4 (December 1900).

Bell, W. Bruce. "The Old Chisholm Trail." *Kiwanis Magazine,* October 1960.

Carley, Maurine. "Salt Wells." *Annals of Wyoming* 34, No. 2 (October 1962).

Dodge, Maj. Gen. Grenville M. "Biographical Sketch of James Bridger." *Annals of Wyoming* 33, No. 2 (October 1961).

Gooch, Hunter W. "The Overland Mail Company—A Long Route." *Golden West Magazine,* April 1975.

Harris, Earl R. "Courthouse and Jail Rocks." *Nebraska History* 43, No. 1 (March 1962).

Howard, Robert West. "South Pass: Gateway of Manifest Destiny." *Westerners Brand Book* (Chicago Corral) 20, No. 2 (April 1963).

Jackson, William Turrentine. "Western Military Roads." *Westerners Brand Book* (Chicago Corral) 14, No. 10 (December 1947).

Klement, Frank L. "Mormons in the Trans-Mississippi West, 1837–1860." *Westerners Brand Book* (Chicago Corral) 25, No. 12 (February 1969).

McKinstry, Bruce L. "Tracing the Trail of California Gold Rush." *Westerners Brand Book* (Chicago Corral) 32, No. 7 (November 1975).

Nute, Grace Lee. "The Red River Trails." *Minnesota History* 6 (September 1925).

"A Panoply of Western Transportation." *Oklahoma Today,* Autumn 1968.

Rhodes, Lynwood Mark. "Life on the Western Wagon Trails." *American Legion Magazine,* January 1971.

Robinson, W. W. "Meanwhile, Back at the Ranchos." *Westways* 58, No. 10 (October 1966).

Simplich, Frederich. "The Santa Fe Trail, Path to Empire." *National Geographic,* August 1929.

Smith, Waddell F. "Waddell F. Smith on the Pony Express." *Westerners Brand Book* (Chicago Corral) 22, No. 11 (January 1966).

"Stage Lines." *Butterfield Express* 4, No. 3 (January 1966).

Terry, F. H. "Across the Rockies in Fifty-Two." *Southwest Virginia Enterprise* (Wytheville, Va.), February 5, 1929.

Tree Planters (Auburn, Neb.) 4, No. 1 (July 1897).

"Weather Fair But Rather Windy." *Journal* (The Mullan Trail, Part 3; Ritzville, Wash.), May 10, 1956.

Wiltsey, Norman B. "First Navigator of the Prairies." *Frontier Times,* Spring 1959.

BOOKS

Abbott, Edward C., and Smith, Helena H. *We Pointed Them North: Recollections of a Cowpuncher.* New York, 1939.

Adams, Ramon F. *Western Words: A Dictionary of the American West.* Norman, Okla., 1975.

Adams, William Bridges. *English Pleasure Carriages.* London, 1837.

American Heritage, Editors of. *The American Heritage History of the Great West.* New York, 1965.

———. *Great Adventures of the Old West.* New York, 1969.

Angle, Paul M. *The American Reader.* Chicago, 1958.

Athearn, Robert G. *High Country Empire.* Lincoln, Neb., 1967.

———, and Riegel, Robert E. *America Moves West.* New York, 1964.

Bari, Valeska. *The Course of Empire.* New York, 1931.

Barns, Cass G. *The Sod House.* Lincoln, Neb., 1970.

Beal, Merrill D. *The Story of Man in Yellowstone.* Caldwell, Idaho, 1949.

Billington, Ray Allen. *The Far Western Frontier: 1830–1860.* New York, 1956.

———, and Ridge, Martin, eds. *America's Frontier Story: A Documentary History of Westward Expansion.* New York, 1969.

Block, Eugene B. *Great Stagecoach Robbers of the West.* Garden City, N.Y., 1962.

Bradley, Glenn Danford. *The Story of the Santa Fe.* Boston, 1920.

Branch, Edward Douglas. *The Cowboy and His Interpreters.* New York, 1926.

———. *Westward: The Romance of the American Frontier.* New York, 1930.

Britt, Albert. *Toward the Western Ocean: The Story of the Men Who Bridged the Continent, 1803–1869.* Barre, Mass., 1963.

Brooks, Emerson M. *The Growth of a Nation.* New York, 1956.

Brown, Ralph H. *Historical Geography of the United States.* New York, 1948.

Brown, Robert L. *An Empire of Silver: A History of the San Juan Silver Rush.* Caldwell, Idaho, 1965.

Burt, Maxwell Struthers. *Powder River.* New York, 1938.

Burton, Sir Richard. *The Look of the West, 1860.* Lincoln, Neb., 1963.

Calvin, Ross. *Sky Determines: An Interpretation of the Southwest.* Albuquerque, N.M., 1966.

Casey, Robert J. *The Texas Border, and Some Borderliners.* Indianapolis, 1950.

Caughey, John Walton. *California.* Englewood Cliffs, N.J., 1953.

Clark, Thomas D. *Frontier America.* New York, 1959.

Clayton, William. *William Clayton's Journal.* Salt Lake City, 1921.

Clowser, Don C. *Deadwood—The Historic City.* Deadwood, S.D., 1969.

Cole, Harry Ellsworth. *Stage Coach and Tavern Tales of the Old Northwest.* Edited by Louise Phelps Kellogg. Cleveland, 1930.

Collins, Ivan L. *Horse Power Days: Popular Vehicles of*

Nineteenth Century America. Stanford, Calif., 1953.

Conard, Howard Louis. *Uncle Dick Wootton.* Chicago, 1957.

Conkling, Margaret B., and Conkling, Roscoe P. *The Butterfield Overland Mail 1857–1869.* Glendale, Calif., n.d.

Corle, Edwin, *Desert Country.* New York, 1941.

———. *The Royal Highway.* Indianapolis, 1949.

Cromie, Alice. *Tour Guide to the Old West.* New York, 1976.

Culmer, Frederic Arthur. *A New History of Missouri.* Mexico, Mo., 1938.

Dale, Harrison Clifford, ed. *The Ashley-Smith Explorations and the Discovery of a Central Route to the Pacific, 1822–1829.* Glendale, Calif., 1941.

Dana, Julian. *The Sacramento: River of Gold.* New York, 1939.

Davis, Jean. *Shallow Diggin's: Tales from Montana's Ghost Towns.* Caldwell, Idaho, 1962.

Davis, William Heath. *Seventy-Five Years in California.* Edited by Douglas S. Watson. San Francisco, 1929.

De Voto, Bernard. *Across the Wide Missouri.* Boston, 1947.

———. *The Year of Decision: 1846.* Boston, 1943.

Dick, Everett N., ed. *Tales of the Frontier: From Lewis and Clark to the Last Roundup.* Lincoln, Neb., 1964.

Dorset, Phyllis Flanders. *The New Eldorado.* New York, 1970.

Drago, Harry Sinclair. *Roads to Empire: The Dramatic Conquest of the American West.* New York, 1968.

Dunbar, Seymour. *A History of Travel in America.* Indianapolis, 1915.

Dunlop, Richard. *Doctors of the American Frontier.* Garden City, N.Y., 1965.

———. *Great Trails of the West.* Nashville, Tenn., 1971.

Eggenhofer, Nicholas. *Wagons, Mules and Men: How the Frontier Moved West.* New York, 1961.

Ehrenberg, Hermann. *With Milam and Fannin: Adventures of a German Boy in Texas' Revolution.* Translated by Charlotte Churchill; edited by Henry Smith. Dallas, 1935.

Emory, W. H. *Notes of a Military Reconnaissance from Fort Leavenworth in Missouri to San Diego in California.* Washington, D.C., 1848.

Farnham, Thomas J. *Travels in the Great Western Prairies, the Anhuac and the Rocky Mountains, and in the Oregon Territory.* New York, 1843.

Farrell, Cliff. *The Mighty Land.* Garden City, N.Y., 1975.

Faulk, Odie B. *Destiny Road: The Gila Trail and the Opening of the Southwest.* New York, 1973.

Fergusson, Harvey. *Rio Grande.* New York, 1967.

Fletcher, John Baylis. *Up the Trail in '79.* Norman, Okla., 1968.

G. and D. Cook and Co.'s *Illustrated Catalogue of Carriages and Special Business Advertiser.* Foreword by Paul H. Downing. New York, 1970.

Gage, Jack R. *Wyoming Afoot and Horseback.* Cheyenne, Wyo., 1966.

Garcia, Andrew. *Tough Trip Through Paradise, 1878–1879.* Edited by Bennett H. Stein. Boston, 1967.

Gard, Wayne. *The Chisholm Trail.* Norman, Okla., 1954.

Garrard, Lewis H. *Wah-To-Yah and the Taos Trail.* Norman, Okla., 1955.

Goetzmann, William H. *Exploration and Empire.* New York, 1966.

Greever, William S. *The Bonanza West: The Story of the Western Mining Rushes 1848–1900.* Norman, Okla., 1968.

Gregg, Josiah. *The Commerce of the Prairies.* New York, 1844.

Gries, Tom, and Thomas, Bob. *Will Penny.* New York, 1968.

Grinnell, George Bird. *The Passing of the Great West.* Edited by John F. Reiger. New York, 1972.

Griswold, Don, and Griswold, Jean. *Colorado's Century of "Cities."* 1958.

Haley, James Evetts. *Fort Concho and the Texas Frontier.* San Angelo, Tex., 1952.

———. *The XIT Ranch of Texas.* Chicago, 1929.

Hammond, George P., and Rey, Agapito. *The Rediscovery of New Mexico, 1580–1594.* Albuquerque, N.M., 1967.

Hansen, Harry, and Federal Writers' Project, eds. *Colorado: A Guide to the Highest State.* New York, 1970.

Hastings, Lansford W. *The Emigrant's Guide to Oregon and California.* Cincinnati, 1845.

Havighurst, Walter. *Upper Mississippi: A Wilderness Saga.* New York, 1937.

Hawgood, John A. *America's Western Frontiers: The Exploration and Settlement of the Trans-Mississippi West.* New York, 1967.

Hewitt, James, ed. *Eye-Witnesses to Wagon Trains West.* New York, 1974.

Horan, James D. *Across the Cimarron* [the life story of George Bolds]. New York, 1956.

Horgan, Paul. *Great River: The Rio Grande in North American History.* 2 vols. New York, 1954.

Howard, Robert West, ed. *This Is the West.* Chicago, 1957.

Inman, Col. Henry. *The Old Santa Fe Trail.* Topeka, Kans., 1914.

Jackson, Clarence S., ed. *Picture Maker of the Old West: William H. Jackson.* New York, 1947.

Jackson, William Turrentine. *Wagon Roads West.* New Haven, Conn., 1965.

Johnson, Dorothy M. *The Bloody Bozeman: The Perilous Trail to Montana's Gold.* New York, 1971.

Jones, Evan. *The Minnesota: Forgotten River.* New York, 1962.

Katz, William Loren. *The Black West.* Garden City, N.Y., 1971.

Kenner, Charles L. *A History of New Mexican-Plains Indian Relations.* Norman, Okla., 1969.

Keyes, Nelson Beecher. *The American Frontier: Our*

Unique Heritage. Garden City, N.Y., 1955.

Klasner, Lily. *My Girlhood Among Outlaws*. Edited by Eve Ball. Tucson, Ariz., 1972.

La Farge, Oliver. *Santa Fe: The Autobiography of a Southwestern Town*. Norman, Okla., 1959.

Lavender, David S. *Westward Vision: The Story of the Oregon Trail*. New York, 1963.

Lewis, Lloyd, and Pargellis, Stanley M., eds. *Granger Country*. Boston, 1949.

Lillard, Richard G. *Desert Challenge: An Interpretation of Nevada*. New York, 1942.

Linford, Velma. *Wyoming: Frontier State*. Denver, 1947.

Look, Editors of. *The Santa Fe Trail*. New York, 1946.

Loomis, Noel M. *Wells Fargo*. New York, 1968.

Lowe, Frank. *Mining Camps and Ghost Towns*. Los Angeles, 1974.

Lowe, Percival G. *Five Years a Dragoon*. Norman, Okla., 1965.

McDowell, Bart. *The American Cowboy in Life and Legend*. Washington, D.C., 1972.

McKee, Russell. *The Last West: A History of the Great Plains of North America*. New York, 1974.

McKinstry, Byron N. *The California Gold Rush Overland Diary of Byron N. McKinstry*. Edited by Bruce L. McKinstry. Glendale, Calif., 1975.

McReynolds, Edwin C. *Missouri: A History of the Crossroads State*. Norman, Okla., 1962.

Magoffin, Susan Shelby. *Down the Santa Fe Trail and into Mexico*. Edited by Stella M. Drumm. New Haven, Conn., 1962.

Majors, Alexander. *Seventy Years on the Frontier*. Chicago, 1906.

Marcy, Randolph B. *The Prairie Traveler*. New York, 1859.

Marshall, James. *Santa Fe: The Railroad That Built an Empire*. New York, 1945.

Mathews, Mitford M., ed. *A Dictionary of Americanisms on Historical Principles*. Chicago, 1951.

Mattes, Merrill J. *The Great Platte River Road*. Lincoln, Neb., 1969.

Meeker, Ezra. *Personal Experiences on the Old Oregon Trail Sixty Years Ago*. Seattle, 1912.

Mitchell, Broadus. *American Adventure*. New York, 1949.

Monaghan, Jay. *The Overland Trail*. Freeport, N.Y., 1971.

Moody, Ralph. *Stagecoach West*. New York, 1967.

Moorhead, Max L. *New Mexico's Royal Road: Trade and Travel on the Chihuahua Trail*. Norman, Okla., 1958.

Morgan, Dale L. *The Humboldt, Highroad of the West*. New York, 1943.

Morison, Samuel Eliot. *The Oxford History of the American People*. New York, 1965.

————; Commager, Henry Steele; and Leuchtenburg, William E. *The Growth of the American Republic*, vol. 2. New York, 1969.

Morris, Richard B., and Woodress, James L., eds. *The Westward Movement, 1832–1889*. Saint Louis, 1961.

Nadeau, Reml A. *Fort Laramie and the Sioux Indians*. Englewood Cliffs, N.J., 1967.

Nason, Thelma C. *No Golden Cities*. New York, 1971.

Neider, Charles, ed. *The Great West*. New York, 1958.

Nelson, Bruce. *Land of the Dacotahs*. Lincoln, Neb., 1964.

Olmsted, Frederick Law. *Journey Through Texas*. Edited by James Howard. Austin, Tex., 1963.

Paden, Irene D. *Prairie Schooner Detours*. New York, 1952.

Parkman, Francis. *The Oregon Trail*. New York, 1949.

Paxson, Frederic L. *History of the American Frontier, 1763–1893*. Cambridge, Mass., 1924.

Peattie, Donald Culross. *American Heartwood*. Boston, 1949.

Peirson, Erma. *The Mohave River and Its Valley*. Glendale, Calif., 1970.

Perez de Villagia, Gaspar. *A History of New Mexico*. Chicago, 1933.

Perkin, Robert L. *The First Hundred Years: An Informal History of Denver and the Rocky Mountain News*. Garden City, N.Y., 1959.

Philipson, J. *Coach Building*. London, 1896.

Reinhardt, Richard. *Out West on the Overland Train*. Palo Alto, Calif., 1967.

Richardson, Albert D. *Beyond the Mississippi: From the Great River to the Great Ocean*. Hartford, Conn., 1867.

Riesenberg, Felix, Jr. *The Golden Road: The Story of California's Spanish Mission Trail*. New York, 1962.

Rister, Carl Coke. *The Southwestern Frontier—1865–1881*. Cleveland, 1928.

Rittenhouse, Jack D. V. *American Horse-Drawn Vehicles*. Los Angeles, 1951.

Robinson, Elwyn B. *History of North Dakota*. Lincoln, Neb., 1966.

Rollins, Philip A. *The Cowboy: His Characteristics, His Equipment, and His Part in the Development of the West*. New York, 1922.

Rouse, Parke, Jr. *The Great Wagon Road: From Philadelphia to the South*. New York, 1973.

Russell, Donald B. *The Lives and Legends of Buffalo Bill*. Norman, Okla., 1960.

————. *The Wild West: A History of the Wild West Shows*. Fort Worth, Tex., 1970.

Sage, Leland L. *A History of Iowa*. Ames, Iowa, 1974.

Settle, Raymond W., and Settle, Mary Lund, eds. *Overland Days to Montana in 1865, The Diary of Sarah Raymond*. Glendale, Calif., 1971.

Sheridan, Philip H. *Personal Memoirs of P. H. Sheridan*. 2 vols. New York, 1888.

Sickels, Eleanor M. *In Calico and Crinoline: True Stories of American Women, 1608–1865*. Freeport, N.Y., 1971.

Spring, Agnes Wright. *The Cheyenne and Black Hills Stage and Express Routes.* Lincoln, Neb., 1965.

Stegner, Wallace E. *The Gathering of Zion: The Story of the Mormon Trail.* New York, 1964.

Stewart, George R. *The California Trail: An Epic With Many Heroes.* New York, 1962.

Stone, Irving. *Men to Match My Mountains: The Story of the Opening of the Far West 1840–1900.* Garden City, N.Y., 1956.

Streeter, Floyd Benjamin. *The Kaw: The Heart of a Nation.* New York, 1941.

Summerhayes, Martha. *Vanished Arizona: Recollections of My Army Life.* Edited by Milo Milton Quaife. Chicago, 1939.

Tarr, László. *The History of the Carriage.* Translated by Elisabeth Hoch. New York, 1969.

Taylor, Morris F. *First Mail West: Stagecoach Lines on the Santa Fe Trail.* Albuquerque, N.M., 1971.

Thomas, Dana Lee. *The Story of American Statehood.* New York, 1961.

Time-Life Books, Editors of. *Prelude 1870–1900.* New York, 1970.

Towne, Charles Wayland, and Wentworth, Edward Norris. *Shepherd's Empire.* Norman, Okla., 1945.

Townshend, Richard B. *A Tenderfoot in Colorado.* Norman, Okla., 1968.

Transactions of the Thirty-Third Annual Reunion of the Oregon Pioneer Association, June 15, 1905. Portland, Ore., 1906.

Tunis, Edwin. *Wheels: A Pictorial History.* Cleveland, 1955.

Twain, Mark. *Roughing It.* New York, 1913.

200 Years: A Bicentennial Illustrated History of the United States. 2 vols. U.S. News and World Report. Washington, D.C., 1973.

Vestal, Stanley. *Kit Carson: The Happy Warrior of the Old West.* Boston, 1928.

———. *The Missouri.* New York, 1945.

———. *The Old Santa Fe Trail.* Boston, 1939.

Walker, Kenneth R. *A History of the Middle West.* Little Rock, Ark., 1972.

Walton, George. *Sentinel of the Plains: Fort Leavenworth and the American West.* Englewood Cliffs, N.J., 1973.

Warren, Sidney. *Farthest Frontier: The Pacific Northwest.* New York, 1949.

Waters, Lawrence L. *Steel Trails to Santa Fe.* Lawrence, Kans., 1950.

Webb, Todd. *The Gold Rush Trail and the Road to Oregon.* Garden City, N.Y., 1963.

Webb, Walter Prescott. *The Great Plains.* Boston, 1931.

Williams, Albert N. *Rocky Mountain Country.* New York, 1950.

Winther, Oscar Osburn. *The Old Oregon Country: A History of Frontier Trade, Transportation, and Travel.* Stanford, Calif., 1950.

———. *The Transportation Frontier.* New York, 1964.

Index

Canadian River, 20, 27
Canutson, Madame, 108, 109
Canyon Diablo Bridge (Arizona), 184
Carney, Jim, 118
Carpenter, Helen M., 63
Carreta, 11, 18, 19-21, 22-28, 45
Carrington, Henry, 96
Carson, Kit, 38, 39, 58
Carson City, Nevada, 148
Carson wagon, 112
Cart, 29, 58, 166, 171. *See also* Carreta;
    Handcart; Red River cart
Casper, Wyoming, 84, 91
Castaño de Sosa, Gaspar, 20-21, 22, 23, 25
Caster, Daniel, 36
Castillo Guijarros (California), 26
Castroville, Texas, 80
Cattle shipments: by railroad, 167
Celerity wagon, 129, 143
Central Pacific Railroad, 181, 183: con-
    struction of, 181, 183
Chaise, 132
Chamberlain Mine, Idaho Springs, Colo-
    rado, 126
Charles, Tom, 19
Cheyenne, Wyoming, 103, 107, 112-113,
    123, 136, 141, 143, 144, 190
Cheyenne and Black Hills Stage Line, 141
Cheyenne Carriage Works, 129, 144
Cheyenne Daily Leader: and Calamity
    Jane, 108
Cheyenne Indians, 14, 27, 181
Cheyenne Wells, Colorado, 107
Chicago, Illinois: Museum of Science and
    Industry, 135; Newberry Library, 64
Chief Rotten Belly, 56, 57
Chief Turkey Foot, 181
Chinook, Montana, 126
Chip wagon, 171
Chisholm Trail, 167
Chisholm Trail, The (Gard), 167-168
Chisos Mountains, 22
Christian IX of Denmark, 155
Chuck wagon, 166-171, 172: on the trail,
    169, 170-171
Church of Jesus Christ of Latter-day
    Saints. *See* Mormons; Mormon Trail
Ciboleros, 27, 45
Cimarron, New Mexico, 125
Cimarron Cutoff: on Santa Fe Trail, 29,
    37, 38
Clark, William, 45
Clayton, William, 73: journal quoted, 73
Coan and Ten Broeke company, 145
Cochise, 14
Cody, Buffalo Bill, 34, 92, 109-110, 152,
    154, 155: quoted, 34, 109-110
Coldon, Sid, 114, 116
Cold Springs, Oklahoma, 101
Collins, Caspar W., 47, 91
Collins, W. H., 91
Colorado goldfields, 61, 63, 65: and hand-
    carters, 64
Colorado Gold Rush, 63, 64
Colorado Springs, Colorado, 187
Columbia, California, 142
Columbus, Nebraska. *See* Colville
Colville, Nebraska, 152, 154
Comanche Indians, 27

Comancheros, 27, 45
Commerce of the Prairies (Gregg), 35
Commissary wagon. *See* Chuck wagon
Comstock Lode, 103
Conchos River, 24
Concord, New Hampshire, 132, 136, 142
Concord coach, 129, 130-136, 143, 145,
    152: artwork on, 135; chassis, 134;
    shipment by railroad, 142; team, 134.
    See also Stagecoach
Concord Daily Monitor (New Hamp-
    shire): reports on Concord coach, 136,
    142
Conestoga wagon, 11, 29, 29-33, 34, 61,
    89, 90, 97: teamsters, 32, 33-34. *See
    also* Covered wagon
Continental Divide, 45, 46, 48, 121, 133.
    See also South Pass
Conyers, Enoch W., 79
Cooper, Tom, 149
Cooper wagon, 103
Corn freight, 118, 119
Coronado, Francisco Vázquez de, 13, 20
Council Grove, Kansas, 36, 38, 41
Covered wagon, 11, 35, 61, 63-64, 66-67,
    77, 84, 86, 87, 184: coverings, 31, 63-64,
    96-97; on emigrant trails, 67, 73, 74,
    76, 77, 79-80, 82, 83-84, 85, 184; inte-
    rior, 63. *See also* Conestoga wagon;
    Freight wagons; Military escort wag-
    on; Prairie schooner; Six-mule Army
    wagon
Cow: as draft animal, 64, 84
Creigh, Thomas Alfred, 110-111
Cripple Creek, Colorado, 151, 184
Crow Indians, 27
Custard, Amos J., 91
Custer, Elizabeth, 98, 99
Custer, Emmanuel H., 87
Custer, George Armstrong, 87, 92, 95, 98,
    99
Custer Expedition: Black Hills, 95

Dalrymple Farm (Minnesota), 175
Davis, Charles E., 67
Davis, Mort, 86
Davis, Theodore R., 144
Davis, William Heath, 24-25: quoted, 25,
    26-27, 28
Davis, William Watts Hart, 22
Deadwood, South Dakota, 59, 100, 103,
    104, 122, 124, 141
Deadwood stage, 141, 152, 154, 155
Deadwood Trail: wagon train on, 109
Deadwood Treasure Wagon, 155
Dearborn, Henry, 46
Dearborn wagon, 29, 36, 46, 54, 56, 129
Death Valley, California, 103, 104, 105
Death Valley Scotty, 104, 105: wife of,
    104
Decorah, Iowa: Vesterheim (museum),
    165
Del Norte, Colorado, 122
Democrat wagon, 172
Denver, Colorado, 83, 116, 128, 143
Denver & Rio Grande Railroad, 190
Dodge, Grenville, 181, 183
Dodge City, Kansas, 187

Dog: as draft animal, 13, 64
Dolores, Colorado, 161
Donner Party, 67, 75
Dormitory railway cars, 193
Double-deck wagon, 66-67
Dougherty wagon, 92, 98, 99, 100
Downing, Lewis, 132-134, 143
Draft animals, 11, 13, 14, 28, 33-34, 39-
    40, 44, 64, 79, 83-84, 89, 96-97, 103,
    105, 107, 114, 118, 119, 121, 130, 167
Dry Cimarron Ranch (New Mexico), 167
Dubuque, Iowa, 103
Dunbar, Seymour, 30: description of Con-
    estoga wagon, 30
Durant, Thomas C., 181

Eastern Oklahoma Railway: construction
    of, 183
Eaton, Gilbert & Company, 145
Echo Canyon, Utah, 67
Edward, Prince of Wales, 155
Elizabethan Gold Mines, 125
El Paso, Texas. *See* Magoffinsville
Emigrants' handbook, 61: quoted, 61, 79,
    84
Emigrant trails: covered wagons on, 67,
    73, 74, 76, 77, 79-80, 82, 83-84, 85,
    184. *See also* Mormon Trail; Oregon
    Trail; Santa Fe Trail
English stagecoach, 132, 134
Espenscheidt wagon, 29, 103
Excursion service: by stagecoach, 163,
    164, 191
Express service: by railroads, 186; by
    stagecoach, 136, 141, 156; by wagon,
    100, 129
Eye-Witnesses to Wagon Trains West
    (Hewitt), 58

Farming machines, 175
Farm wagon, 29, 34, 44, 61, 130, 165-166,
    171, 172, 173, 175, 177
Fast Horse, David, 13
Fell, Dr. Barry, 14
Fence wagon, 171
Ferguson, William, 22: quoted, 22
Fitzpatrick, Thomas ("Broken Hand"),
    55-56
Five Years a Dragoon (Lowe), 89
Fletcher, Tom, 179
Folsom, California, 179
Fontenelle, Lucien, 53-54
Forbes, J. T., 114, 116
Fort Abraham Lincoln, Dakota Territory,
    92, 95, 98
Fort Atkinson, Kansas, 45
Fort Atkinson, Nebraska, 46
Fort Bayard, New Mexico, 96
Fort Benton, Montana, 103
Fort Boise, Idaho, 56, 57
Fort Bonneville, Wyoming, 48
Fort Bridger, Wyoming, 196
Fort Caspar, Wyoming, 91
Fort Defiance, Arizona, 92
Fort Hall, Idaho, 47, 56, 58
Fort Hoskins, Oregon, 101
Fort Laramie, Wyoming, 47, 53, 58, 66